YOU ARE
STUPID SCUMBAGS WHO EVEN
GOT THEMSELVES
ATTENTION IN PUBLIC.
YOU'RE
THE ONLY HOPE
THAT'S LEFT
ON THIS GODLESS PLANET!

33

LOVE SWEAT AND TEARS

KERBER CULTURE

KILAUEAS
KINK
KLANGKARUSSEL
KLEZ.E
KLEINKARIERT
KNAUGHTY KNIGHTS
KOAN SOUND
KONRAD BLACK
KONRAD KUHN
KONSHENS
KONSTANTIN SIBOLD
KONTAKT
KOOL DJ SWIST
KRAFTY KUTS
KRAUSE DUO
KRAZY BALDHEAD
KRIKOR
KRM
KRIZE
KURTIS BLOW
LADY SAW
LA LOC
LASERKRAFT 3D
LAURA JONES
LAURENT GARNIER
LAWRENCE
LECCO B
LEE BABY SIMM
LEEROY THORNHILL
LEIF MÜLLER
LE PETIT PILOUS
LESOTHO BROTHERS
LEVONT VINCENT
LEXIE LEE
LEXY
LINDSTRØM
LIVIO
LOCO DICE
LOUIE AUSTIN
LORETTA
LOS PORNOS
LTJ BUKEM
LÜTZENKIRCHEN
L-VIS 1990
MÄRTINI BRÖS.
MABIK
MAD MAX
MAETRIK
MAGDA
MAKE THE GIRL DANCE
MALENTE
MANARÉ
M.A.N.D.Y.
MANIK
MANON
MANUEL BÜRGER
MANUEL SCHORN
MARAL SALMASI
MARBERT ROCEL
MARC CALMBACH
MARC FORREST
MARC HOULE
MARC MAUTZ
MARC ROMBOY
MARCEL DETTMANN

MARCEL JANOVSKY
MARCO CAROLA
MARCO ZAFFARANO
MAREK HEMMANN
MARIO KOBER
MARIUS LEHNERT
MARTIN BUTTRICH
MARTIN EYERER
MARKUS GRUND
MARTIN HÖRGER
MARTIN LANDSKY
MARKUS KAVKA
MARKUS LANGE
MARKUS METHA
MARSIMOTO SOUNSYS.
MASSIVE DISCO
MASTER KULA
MATHIAS KADEN
MATTHIAS MEYER
MATTHIAS TANZMANN
MATZE BACH
MATT JOHN
MAX HERRE
MAX PASK
MC CONRAD
MC MAD SKILLZ
MC MANKIND
MC MIKE ROMERO
MC REMEDY
MEDIENGRUPPE TELEK.
MEHDI
METOPE
METRO AREA
MICHAEL MAYER
MICHAEL REINBOTH
MICHI BECK
MIGNON
MIJK VAN DIJK
MIKE MENUDO
MILDRUS
MINILOGUE
MINIMALTE
MINI MOUSTACHE
MISCHINSKI
MISSILL
MISS EVOICE
MISS KITTIN
MISS TABOO
MIXHELL
MODESELEKTOR
MØENSTER
MONIKA KRUSE
MONCHROME
MOPOT
MORITZ VON PEIN
MOTORCITY
DRUM ENSEMBLE
MOUNT SIMS
MOVE D
M-PIPER
MR. FLASH
MR. OIZO
MR. REEDOO
MR. VEGAS
MTMBT

MUALLEM
MUNK
MUTE ME
MY MY
NAKARA
NAMOSH
NHAN SOLO
NATHAN FAKE
ND_BAUMECKER
N-DEE
NEKES
NETZER
NEW JUDAS
NEW YOUNG PONY CLUB
NICKI PAULS
NO CONTROL
NORCUT
NORTHERN LITE
NOSLIW
NU
OAWL
OH HI!
OH SNAP!
OLIVER HAFENBAUER
OLIVER HAUF
OLIVER KOLETZKI
OLLI BANJO
ONUR ÖZER
OPEN MIKE
OPTIMO
ORACY
ORIGINAL SINNERS
OST BLOCKSCHLAMPEN
PABLO VALENTINO
PALINA POWER
PANTHA DU PRINCE
PANTONE
PAPA NOAH
PATRICK KUNKEL
PAUKI
PAUL BRTSCHITSCH
PAULS ARTISTS
PEACHES
PETAR DUNDOV
PFADFINDEREI
PHILIPE DE BOYAR
PHLEGMATIC
PHONIQUE
PHON.O
PILLOWTALK
PINKY N' BRAIN
PIWI
PLAN B
PLANET B.E.N.
PLAY PAUL
POLYMORPHIC
POPULETTE
POW POW SOUNDSYS.
PRESIDENT BONGO
PRINCE LANGUAGE
PROSUMER
PSYCHOZ
PUNKS JUMP UP
PUTTE
QUANTIC

RAM
RAMPA
RAPAHEL DINCSOY
RARESH
RAINER TRÜBY
REBOOT
RED ROBIN
REDSHAPE
REHASH
RENAISSANCE MAN
RESO
REWORK
RE.YOU
RICKY TROOPER
RITON
ROBAG WRUHME
ROBERT BABICZ
ROBERT STADLOBER
ROBIN T. TREIER
ROB BIRCH
ROB MEDINA
ROB LANDO
ROBY
ROCK KRAUS
ROTZE
ROMAN FLÜGEL
ROUND TABLE KNIGHTS
RUB'N TUG
RUEDE HAGELSTEIN
RUPERT SUFKIN
SAINT PAULI
SALAMANDER
SAN GABRIEL
SANTÉ
SASCHA
SASCHA DIVE
SASCHA FUNKE
SASCHA SIBLER
SASSE
SAVAS PASCALIDIS
SCHAEBEN & VOSS
SCHOWI
SENTINEL SOUND
SETH TROXLER
SHAMEBOY
SHED
SHIR KHAN
SHITROBOT
SICK GIRLS
SID DEMON
SIMON BAKER
SILLEX
SILLY WALKS
SIRKRIS
SIS
SKIP JENSEN
SKULLS N' BONES
SLAM
SLEEPER THIEF
SMASH F/X
SMASH TV
SOLOMUN
SOMEONE ELSE
SOMOS
SONO

SONIC ANGELS
SORRY COMPUTER
SOUL CLAP
SOUL GLOW DJ TEAM
SOULPHICTION
SOULWAX
SOUND OF STEREO
SOUNDSTREAM
SNAX
SPIRIT CATCHER
STEPHAN BODZIN
STEREO EXPRESS
STEVE BUG
STEVE LAWLER
STIMMING
STOMPIN' JOHNSON
STONE COLD CRAZY
STONE LOVE
STUPID DEEP
SUBMARIEN
SUGAR HILL GANG
SUGA ROY
SUNSET
SUPERPITCHER
SUPERSONICS
SUPERSUPER
SUZANNA ROSKOZNY
SVEN WEISEMANN
SWAYZAK
SWEET N' CANDY
SYLVIE MARKS
TABI TABOO
TAMARA
TANGO CHOP SUEY
TATOOED MILLIONAIRES
TELEFUNKEN EXPRESS
TENT
TENSNAKE
TERRANOVA
TERRENCE FIXMER
THOMAS LUX
THOMAS MEINECKE
THOMAS SCHUMACHER
THORSTEN W
THE BLOODY BEETROOTS
THE DETECTIVES
THE HACKER
THE GAMBLERS
THE JETSET
THE JIKI JIKI WAH WAHS
THE LOVEMACHINES
THE ODDWORD
THE PROXY
THE S
THE SCANDALS
THE SUBS
THIEVES LIKE US
TIEFSCHWARZ
TIGA
TIGERSHRIMP
TIGERSKIN
TILL KRÜGER
TIM GREEN
TIM SWEENEY
TIMO MAAS

TINI
TIPURA
TKZ
TNT JACKSON
T.O.K.
TOBI NEUMANN
TOBIAS BECKER
TODD BODINE
TOKYO TOWER
TOM DELUXX
TOMAS BARFORD
TOME
TONI RIOS
TONY TOUCH
TOK TOK
TRACKY BIRTHDAY
TRASH MONKEYS
TROLLEY SNATCHA
TROY PIERCE
TRENTEMØLLER
TRICKSKI
TRIPOLD
TRIPPLE ESPRESSO
TRUMPDISCO
TUBE & BERGER
TURBOWEEKEND
TURNTABLEROCKER
TWO DOOR CINEMA
CLUB
UDO QUARTETT
UFFIE
UPLIFTMENT SOUND
URLAUB IN POLEN
VAMPIRE WEEKEND
VICARIOUS BLISS
VINCENZO
VNNR
VJ FREE MIND
VJ FRISCHVERGIFTUNG
VJ KAUNDWON
VJ ONNI POHL
VJ PROLEX
VJ RAUL
VJ REVOLIZER
WAREIKA
WARRIOR SOUND
WATERLILLY
WELTRAUMQUARTETT
WHITE NOISE
WHITEST BOY ALIVE
WHO MADE WHO
WIGHNOMY BROTHERS
WOLF & LAMB
WOODY
WRONGKONG
XANDER
XKORE
YASSIN
YELLE
ZAMARROW
ZERO CASH
ZIEL 100
ZOMBIE DISCO SQUAD
ZOMBIE NATION
ZOOT WOMAN

ROCKE
33

„I stole my sister's boyfriend. It was all whirlwind, heat, and flash. Within a week we killed my parents and hit the road." Sonic Youth

D Um die Jahrtausendwende war poppiger Mainstream House die angesagteste Musik für jede After Work Party in deutschen Großstädten. So auch in Stuttgart. Mit einem Sekt auf Eis in der Hand bewegten sich schöne Agenturmenschen in poshen Läden am kleinen Schloßplatz oder der aufkeimenden Theodor-Heuss-Straße. Die totproduzierte Variante von House war glatt, ohne Ecken und Kanten, weichgespült und absolut massenkompatibel. Überall lief dieselbe Musik, langweilig und entsetzlich mainstreamig.

Das gefiel uns nicht. Inspiriert von Metal, Punk, der DIY-Bewegung, subversiver Mode oder unkonventioneller Kunst wollten wir der Weichspüler-Kultur etwas entgegensetzen. Etwas mit Dreck unter den Fingernägeln, mit Charakter und Patina. Etwas das schmerzt und uns das Leben spüren ließ — in all seinen Facetten. Wir feierten Partys in kleinen, dreckigen Kellern mit selbst gezimmerten Bars, ohne zweiten Fluchtweg und mit fahler Beleuchtung. Wir mischten Punk mit Elektro und nahmen billige Drogen aus Osteuropa. Die Ästhetik der 80er Jahre gefiel uns: selbst machen, verfremden, kopieren und vervielfältigen wie Andy Warhol. Wir gestalteten Sticker und Flyer von Hand und am Computer, klebten, zerschnitten und zerknüllten das Papier, scannten es nochmals ein und kopierten es hundertfach im Copy Shop von Heinz Rocker in der Ludwigstrasse 33. Wir übernahmen das Logo auf der Schaufensterscheibe eins zu eins — ohne ihn jemals gefragt zu haben.

Vor jeder Planungsphase liegt eine der Zeit der Illusion und des Träumens. „Bau dir doch deine eigene Stadt." So muss man denken, sonst bewegt sich nichts. Diese Haltung war auch Grundlage für die Planung und Umsetzung des Rocker 33, der als rauschbeladenes

Konstrukt nicht einmal ansatzweise vergleichbar zur tatsächlichen Form in unseren Köpfen geisterte. Aber wer waren wir überhaupt? Abstrahieren wir: Amateure, Getriebene und Treibende, naive Illusionisten, weltfremde Enthusiasten. So oder so ähnlich fanden wir uns im Jahre 2003 als eine Gruppe Begeisterungsfähiger zusammen, die ihre Vorstellungen von Selbstverwirklichung und Kreationstrieb auf eine gemeinsame Formel zusammendampften: Das Ganze ist immer mehr als die Summe seiner Teile.

Wir sehen uns auf der anderen Seite! Und so fanden wir in den ehemaligen Verkaufsräumen des Music Shop Molu auf dem kleinen Schlossplatz ein kurz vor dem Abriss stehenden Ort, wenn auch nur kurze Zeit, wo Kunst und Exzess, Improvisation und Perfektionismus, Sex und Kalkül aufeinandertrafen. Mitten in der Stadt. Und gerade die Stadtverwaltung war es, die das Projekt zunächst behutsam protegierte. Es gab offizielle Ansprachen, Selbstbeweihräucherung und blamable Situationen, aber am Ende zählte das Ergebnis: ein aus Schweiß, Tränen und schwarzer Farbe angerührter Palast des Rauschs. Und der Kunst. Temporären Projekten haftet stets die Gunst des Verwüstbaren an. Drei Monate, drei Ausstellungen, 3 und noch mal die 3: der Rocker 33 war geboren.

E At the turn of the millennium, trendy mainstream house was the hippest music for any after after-work party in German cities. Same in Stuttgart. With a sparkling wine on ice in hand beautiful agency people moved in posh bars at the Kleiner Schloßplatz or the upcoming Theodor-Heuss-Straße. The boring variant of house music was smooth, without corners and edges, softened and completely mass-compatible. Everywhere the same music was served, uninspired and horribly dull.

We didn't not that. Inspired by metal, punk, the DIY movement, subversive fashion or unconventional art, we wanted to shape a counter part to the mainstream culture. Something dirty, with character and patina.

Something that hurts and made us feel real life — in all its aspects. We celebrated parties in small, dirty cellars with self-made bars, no second escape route and with dimmed lighting. We mixed punk with electro and took cheap drugs from Eastern Europe. We liked the aesthetics of the 80s: handmade, alienated, copied and duplicated like Andy Warhol did. We designed stickers and flyers by hand and on the computer, pasted, cut and crumpled up the paper, scanned it again and copied it hundreds of times in the copy shop of Heinz Rocker in Ludwigstrasse 33. We took the logo on the shop window one to one — without ever having asked him.

Before each prepping phase there is the time of illusion and dreaming. „Build your own city." Think like that, otherwise would won't move nothing at all. This attitude was the basis for the planning and implementation of the Rocker 33, which haunted as a blustery construct not even remotely comparable to the actual shape in our minds. But who were we anyway? Let's put it like that: amateurs, driven and impulsive, naive illusionists, out-of-world enthusiasts. So in 2003, we came together as a group of enthusiasts who combined their ideas of self-realization and its creative energy into a common formula: the whole is always more than the sum of its parts.

We'll see you on the other side! In the former sales rooms of the Music Shop Molu nearby Kleiner Schlossplatz we found a place shortly before its break down. Only for a short time, where art and excess, improvisation and perfectionism, sex and calculation would meet. In the middle of the city. And it was exactly the city administration who initially gently protected the project. There were official speeches, self-congratulations and blamable situations, but in the end is was the result that counted: a palace of intoxication touched with sweat, tears and black paint. And art. Temporary projects always have the favor of the destructible. Three months, three exhibitions, 3 and again the 3: the Rocker 33 was born.

IT'S TIME TO
PRESS THE ...!

D Ob Zufall, Glück oder Schicksal den entscheiden Teil dazu beitrug, dass sich dieser eine Ort in der alten und längst verlassenen Zentrale der Deutschen Bahn in der Heilbronner Straße 7, direkt neben dem Hauptbahnhof finden ließ, wurde nie geklärt. Fakt ist, dass in der ehemaligen Druckerei der Bahndirektion in dem über hundertjährigen Gebäude genug Raum für eine Galerie, eine großzügige Tanzfläche und eine ausladende Bar war. Der große Raum fasste etwa 600 Besucher. Daneben gab es einen kleineren Raum für 150 Gäste — den zukünftigen Mini Club. Und dann gab es noch einen riesigen, verwilderten Innenhof. Und ein prachtvolles Foyer. Und ein ehemaliges Casino im siebten Stock. Und unzählige herrschaftliche Büro-räume. Und … Klingt perfekt? Tja, keine dieser Flächen war auch nur ansatzweise direkt nutzbar. Jemanden zu bezahlen, der alles „baurechtsamtskonform" umbauen konnte, war ausgeschlossen. Und wir selbst hatten keine Ahnung von Umbau. Also legten wir los.

Mit der Kraft unserer Hände und einer ungesunden Portion Naivität rissen wir Mauern ein, legten Strom-leitungen, zimmerten eine Bar zusammen, strichen Gänge, Wände und Decken schwarz und verbrei-terten Fluchtwege. Den hinteren Teil des Gebäudes, in dem sich der Club befinden sollte, und den Innenhof, der zur Entfluchtung dienen musste, trennte eine 90 Zentimeter dicke Wand. Und zwar keine Investoren-Schnellbau-Pappwand, sondern eine massive Vorkriegs-ich-bin-für-die-Ewigkeit-Wand. Zwei Durchbrüche mussten geschaffen werden. Das Mittel unserer Wahl dazu war ein Bohrmeißel von Hilti, den wir nach kurzer Zeit nur noch den „Zorn Gottes" nannten. Abwechselnd bohrten und meißelten wir uns fünf Tage lang Zenti-meter für Zentimeter den Weg frei in den Innenhof, die Schleimhäute komplett verstaubt und ausgetrocknet, die Ohren dröhnten vom Lärm und die Muskeln schmerzten vor Anstrengung — das Hämmern verfolgte uns in unseren Träumen.

Aber der Innenhof war auch nicht nutzbar. Sträucher, Hecken und Bäume machten das Durchkommen unmöglich. Also rodeten wir den Hof bis auf die Wurzeln kurz und klein und jagten alles durch einen gigantischen Häcksler. Wir waren im Rausch. Zerstören, um etwas Neues zu erschaffen. Diesen magischen Ort der Vergangenheit mit roher Gewalt entreißen. In unserem Umbauwahn waren wir irgendwann so im Strudel gefangen, dass wir zuerst gar nicht bemerkten, dass jemand einen Bagger bestellt hatte, der im Innenhof ein riesiges Loch für einen Swimmingpool ausheben sollte. Dabei hatte der Hof eine Erddecke von höchstens zwei Metern und darunter kamen direkt die Kellergeschosse! So musste der Bagger ohne zum Einsatz gekommen zu sein von der Baufirma unverrichteter Dinge wieder abgeholt werden …

Nach Tagen, Wochen und Monaten des Umbaus, Abrisses und Zusammendengelns, nach zahlreichen verschlissenen Werkzeugen und Körperteilen öffnete der „neue" Rocker in allerletzter Minute die verstaubten Pforten — und ließ eine geduldig wartende Menschenmasse ein. Zum Glück blieben in dieser Nacht die installierten Provisorien stehen. Für uns änderte sich nach dieser Nacht aber alles.

E Whether coincidence, luck or fate contributed to the decisive part, that this place in the old and long-abandoned headquarters of the Deutsche Bahn in Heilbronner Straße 7, was found right next to the main station, was never clarified. In fact, at the former printing office of the railway directorate in the over one hundred-year-old building there was enough space for a gallery, a spacious dance floor and a large bar. The big room held about 600 visitors. In addition, there was a smaller room for 150 guests — the future Mini Club. And then there was a huge, overgrown courtyard. And a magnificent foyer. And a former casino on the seventh floor. And countless stately offices. And … sounds perfect? Well, none of these areas was even close to direct use. For us it was impossible to pay someone who was able to convert everything „according to official building regulations". And we ourselves had no idea about conversion. So we started.

With the strength of our hands and an unhealthy dose of naivety, we tore down walls, laid power lines, built a bar, painted corridors, walls and ceilings black, and broadened escape routes. The back of the building where the club was supposed to be, and the courtyard that had to be used for evacuation, separated a 90-centimeter-thick wall. And not cheap thin wall, but a massive I-am-here-to-stay wall. Two breakthroughs had to be made. The means of our choice was a drill bit by Hilti, which we called the „Anger of God". We took turns drilling and carving our way through the courtyard, inch by inch, the mucous membranes completely dusty and dehydrated, our ears roaring with the noise and the muscles aching with the effort — the hammering haunting our dreams.

But the courtyard was not usable neither. Shrubs, hedges and trees made getting through impossible. So we cleared the yard down to the roots and chased everything through a gigantic shredder. We were in a frenzy. Destroy to create something new. Rip this magical place of the past with brute force. In our rebuilding delusion, we were at some point so hooked, that we did not notice that someone had ordered an excavator, which was supposed to dig an enormous hole for a swimming pool in the inner courtyard. The yard had a ceiling of maximum two meters and beneath there was the basement floor! So the excavator had to be picked up again by the construction company without being used …

After days, weeks and months of rebuilding, demolition and congealing, after many worn tools and body parts, the „new" Rocker 33 opened its dusty gates at the last minute — and let in a patiently waiting crowd. Luckily, the temporary restorations installed stayed that night. But everything else changed drastically for us.

YOPK

ON HIRE FROM
matt snowball
music
+44 (0)20 7700 6665

FOR FREE ENTRY
SIGN UP AT
WWW.VICELIVE.DE
PRÄSENTIERT
VICE LIVE
THUNDERHEIST
LITTLE BOOTS
THECOCKNBULLKID
MICKEY MOONLIGHT
13.12. ROCKER33
FREE TICKETS UND MEHR INFOS
UNTER WWW.VICELIVE.DE

Jacob Dove Basker

tech rider:
2 technics turntables
1 pioneer mixer djm 500 or 600
1 shure sm58 or equivalent
1 tisch mit platz für alles plus laptop dazu
2 monitor boxen
freie stromsteckerplätze
a sound engineer that knows the club and can help me. preferably also to mix the sound
and the microphone during the show. if possible.

dann bräuchte ich dazu noch:
12 importierte biere
4 kisten s.pellegrino
1 fernseher mit kabel
1 playstation mit die neusten spiele
4 kilo raw steaks in herzenform geschnitten
1 smith and wesson longbarrel .44 verchromt mit 38 special patronen
1 poster von Keanu Reeves
3 gutaussehende nutten, eine schwarze eine asiatin und eine blondine die zu alles
bereit sind
3 kilo geschälten m&ms, aber nur die die mal grün waren bevor die geschält waren (kein
tricks, das kann ich erkennen!)
1 indische swami die immer neue räucherstäbchen anzündet. er muss aber yogameister
sein.
40 schwarze mullsäcke
1 eigene drogenlabor und chemiestudent der immer customized cocktails für mich
herstellen kann nach meine momentane verfassung
1 privat hubschrauber für zwischen hotel und arena

ich hoffe das ist alles kein problem.
falls mir noch was einfällt sage ich bescheid.
falls was nicht geht sag bescheid. ich bin flexibel.

jake

On 06.04.2005, at 15:34, Thorsten Neumann wrote:

Hallo ich bräuchte deinen vollen Namen damit wir die Tickets reservieren können.
Und schick bitte noch deinen technical rider.
Gruss Thorsten
Am 06.04.2005 um 15:08 schrieb jake@jakelovesyou.com:

21-FEB-2008 12:37   S.01

hi thorsten!

ich brauche:
kleines tisch auf der buehne,
kleines mischpult (4 channel)
cd spieler (beide auf der buehne!)
1 micro
microstand
1 monitor

PART OF THE WEEK END

NEVER DIES

I'LL
BRING
YOU
FLOWERS
IN THE
POURING
RAIN

Life without you is driving me insane.

Stacker
ow's she
ttin'?

NAMOSH

STEVE MORELL

anything

BOY FROM BRAZIL

DAVID GILMORE GIRLS

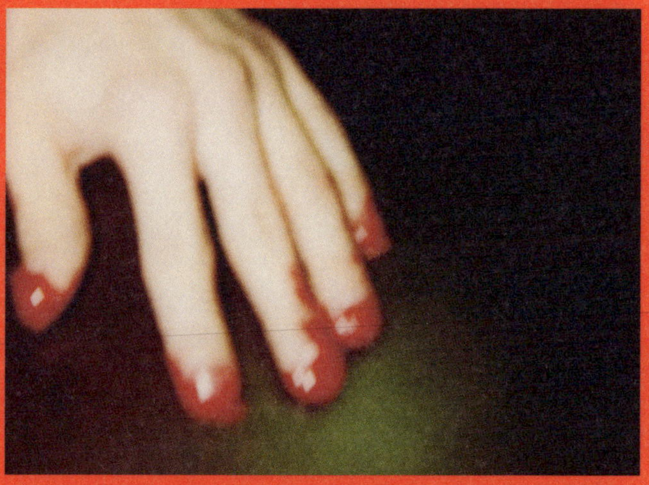

LOSOUL
FEAT. WHITE
x WARRIORS

EROBIQUE

WHEN I
ROCK
THE
PARTY
YOU
BUST
A NUT

Cocaine
KODAK 160NC-2
43
KODAK 160

UFFIE

D Gäste kommen erwartungsvoll, gehen glücklich
oder enttäuscht. Damit das geschehen kann, muss
irgendetwas zwischen Eingang und Ausgang passieren.
Und genau dafür waren wir zuständig. Damit die Leute,
die doch zahlreich kommen sollen, von dem Abend,
der Party oder dem Programm erfahren. Damit sie
den Eingang finden, ihren Eintritt bezahlen können oder
ihren Namen auf der Gästeliste finden können. Damit
sie sich nicht auf dem Weg vom Eingang durch den
Innenhof zum Club verletzen, damit sie eine Musik gebo-
ten bekommen, die sie inspiriert, zum Tanzen bringt
oder zum Bleiben bewegt. Damit sie an der Bar bedient
werden und dass sie viel von dem trinken, das sie
zu glücklich besoffenen Besuchern macht. Für all das
braucht es Menschen, die mehr Gründe haben ihre
Aufgabe gut zu machen, als nur die reine Bezahlung
ihres Stundenlohns. Die Menschen die im und vor allem
für den Rocker 33 gearbeitet haben, haben dies nicht
immer nur aus Leidenschaft getan. Aber doch meistens.
Die Mitarbeiter wollten vor allem mit viel Spaß ihre
Nächte opfern und gerne ihre Zeit mit den Kollegen
an der Tür, der Bar oder hinter dem DJ Pult verbringen.
Sich dabei wie eine große Familie fühlen.

Mit am schwierigsten ist die Besetzung der Türsteher, die über die perfekte Mischung an Gästen und
eine friedliche Nacht mitentscheiden. Und weil es
allen Clubs in einer kleinen Stadt wie Stuttgart damit
gleich geht, sind freundliche, diplomatische und entschie-
dene Bouncer sehr rar. Zunächst helfen Freunde aus,
dann muss man auf Empfehlungen vertrauen. Auf
eigene Erfahrungen kann man aber dabei niemals verzich-
ten. So trat eines Tages ein großer, stets braunge-
brannter und muskulöser Kerl in unseren Dienst, der
mit seiner sanften Stimme und klugen Lebensweisheiten
schnell Vertrauen schaffte. Nicht nur die fernöstliche
Kampfkunst, sondern auch die Religion hatte es ihm

angetan. Wir waren sehr zufrieden, bis wir „Geschichten"
von Gästen hörten. So soll der nette Türsteher mit
dem glatt rasierten Kopf immer wieder ausgerastet sein
und Gäste angegriffen haben. Den Beinamen „Prügel-
buddhist" haben ihm seine Kollegen gegeben. Irgendwann
mussten wir uns von ihm trennen.

Aus einem ganz anderen Holz waren die Mongolen
geschnitzt. Ein mongolischer Politikstudent, zwei
Meter groß und 110 Kilo schwer, hatte sich auf die
Anzeige beworben, in der wir Abräumer gesucht haben.
Das sind zähe Jungs, die auch im größten Getümmel wie
auf Schienen leere Gläser und Flaschen aus dem Club
schaffen und die Kühlschränke wieder auffüllen.
Mugghi kam immer pünktlich, hat sich nie beschwert
und gearbeitet wie eine Maschine. Auch einige seiner
Kommilitonen haben wir eingestellt — stille, aber sym-
pathische Jungs, die die Gästeschar stets um einen Kopf
überragten und sich allein durch ihre stattliche Körper-
fülle einen respektvollen Platz im Club verschafften.
Die Mongolen waren cool. Irgendwann haben sie auch als
Türsteher ausgeholfen und auch hier einen super Job
gemacht. Mugghi war ihr Anführer. Niemand trug die
Rocker-33-Türsteher-Collegejacken würdevoller als die
Mongolen. Nach dem Studium sind die Mongolen längst
wieder in die Mongolei zurückgekehrt und Mugghi ist
heute Präsidentschaftskandidat der Sozialistischen
Partei. Wir sind in Kontakt.

E Guests arrive expectantly, happy or disappointed.
For this to happen, something has to occur between
entrance and exit. And that's exactly what we were
responsible for. Promoting the event so people would
come in large numbers. For guests to find the entrance,
pay their entry or find their name on the guest list.
So they don't hurt themselves on the way from the
entrance through the courtyard to the club, so they can
listen to music that inspires them, music that makes
them want to dance and stay. For everybody to
be served at the bar and to have as many drinks as
make them happy drunk guests. All of these processes
require people who have more reasons to do their job

well than just getting paid by hour. The people who worked in — and above all for — Rocker 33 did not always do this out of passion. But mostly. Usually, the staff wanted to sacrifice their nights and spend their time with colleagues at the door, the bar or behind the DJ desk. To feel like a big family.

The most difficult part is the casting of the doormen, who decide on the perfect mix of guests to guarantee a peaceful night. And because all clubs in a small city like Stuttgart have the same issue, friendly, diplomatic and decisive bouncers are very rare. At first, friends would help out, then you'd have to trust recommendations. But you can never do without your own experience. So one day, a tall, always tanned and muscular guy came into our service, who quickly created confidence with his gentle voice and profound wisdom gained not only Far Eastern martial arts, but also from religion. We were very satisfied until we heard „stories" from guests. So the nice bouncer with the clean-shaven head was said to have attacked guests for no reason. The nickname „beat up buddhist" was given to him by his colleagues. At some point we had to part with him.

The Mongols were carved out of completely different wood. A Mongolian political student, two meters high and weighing 110 kilograms, had applied to an ad in which we were looking for a bar runner. These are tough guys who get empty glasses and bottles from the club and refill the refrigerators even in the biggest fuss like on rails. Mugghi always arrived punctually, never complained and worked like a machine. We also hired some of his fellow students — quiet, but likable guys who always towered over the crowd by a head and managed to find a respectful place in the club just by their stature. The Mongols were cool. At some point they also helped out as bouncers and did a great job here as well. Mugghi was their leader. Nobody wore the Rocker 33 bouncer college jackets in a more dignified way than the Mongols. After graduation, the Mongols have returned to Mongolia and today Mugghi is a presidential candidate of the Socialist Party. We are still in contact.

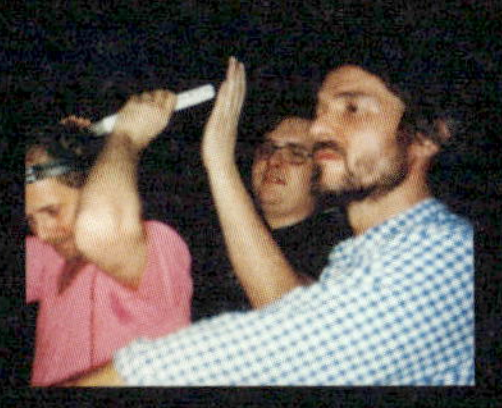

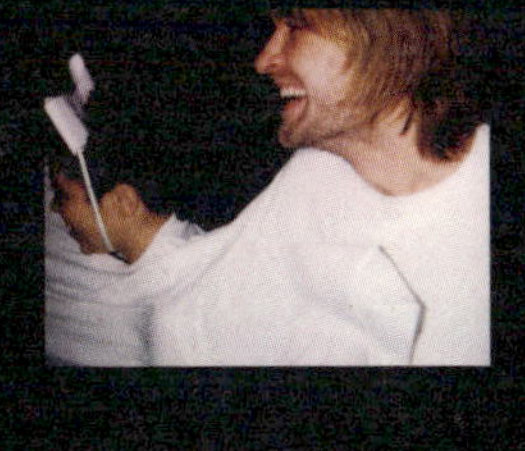

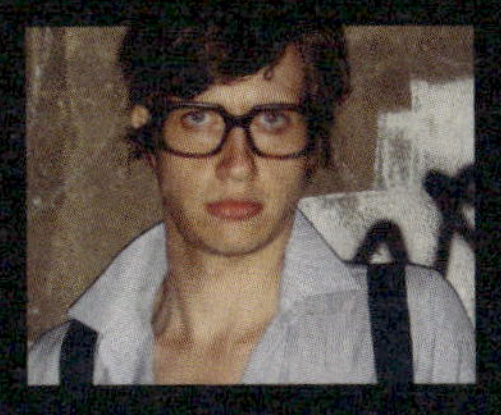

PEACHES

GIVE
RESPECT
STAY HEAL

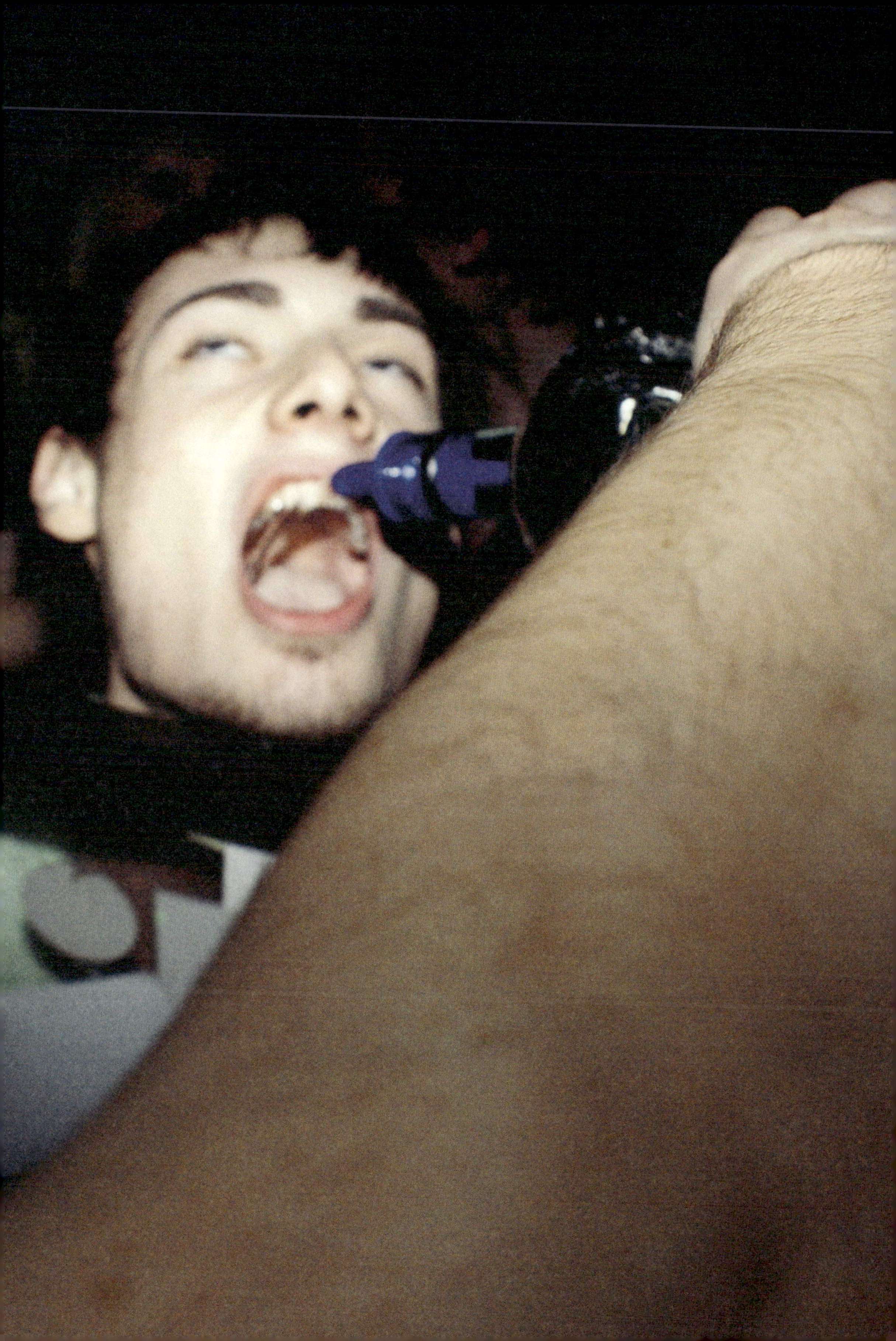

SEALED IN A BAG

SOLD IT BACK TO YOU

JEPPE KJELLBERG (WHOMADEWHO)

STEFF

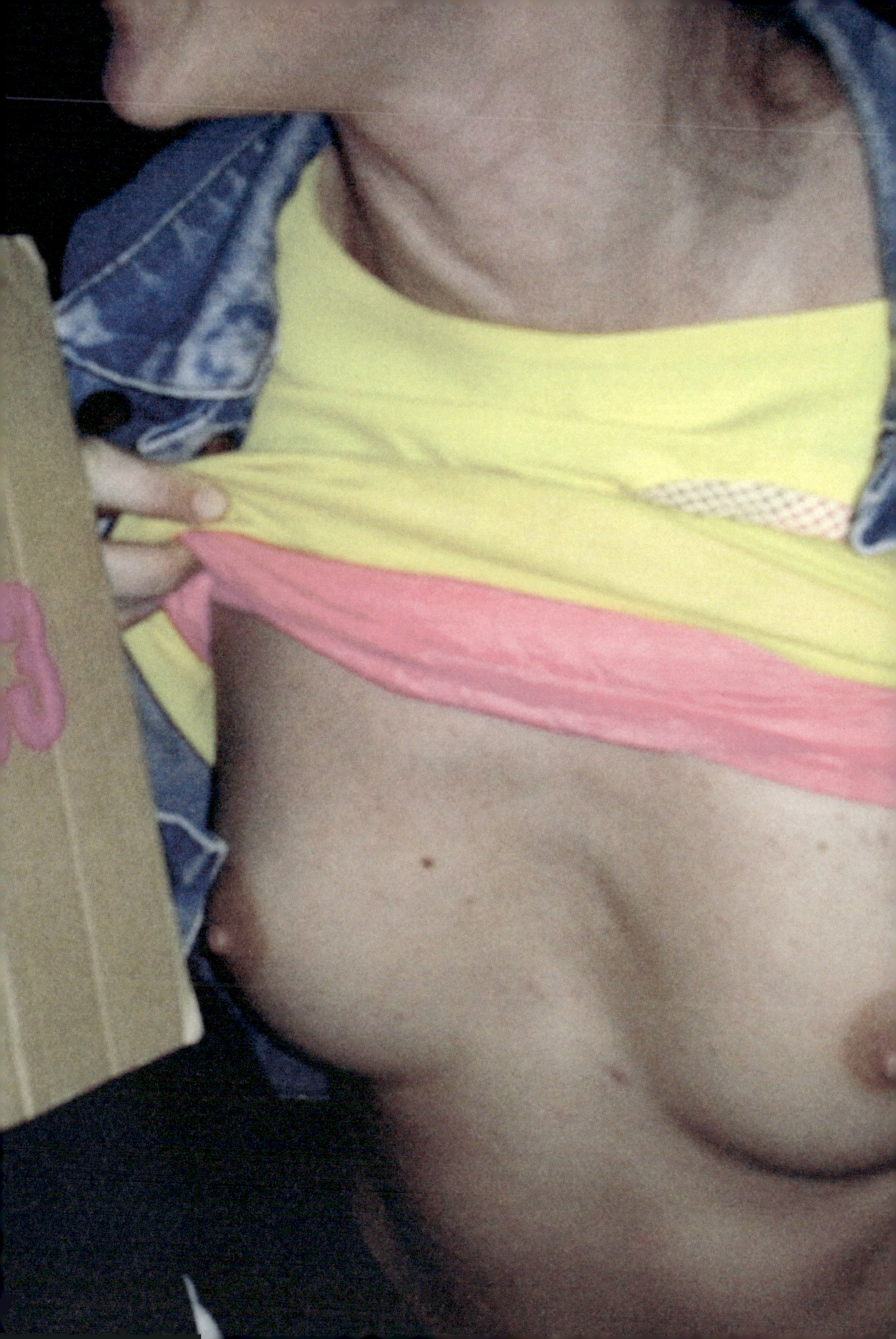

ARK

MATTHIAS & PEJO

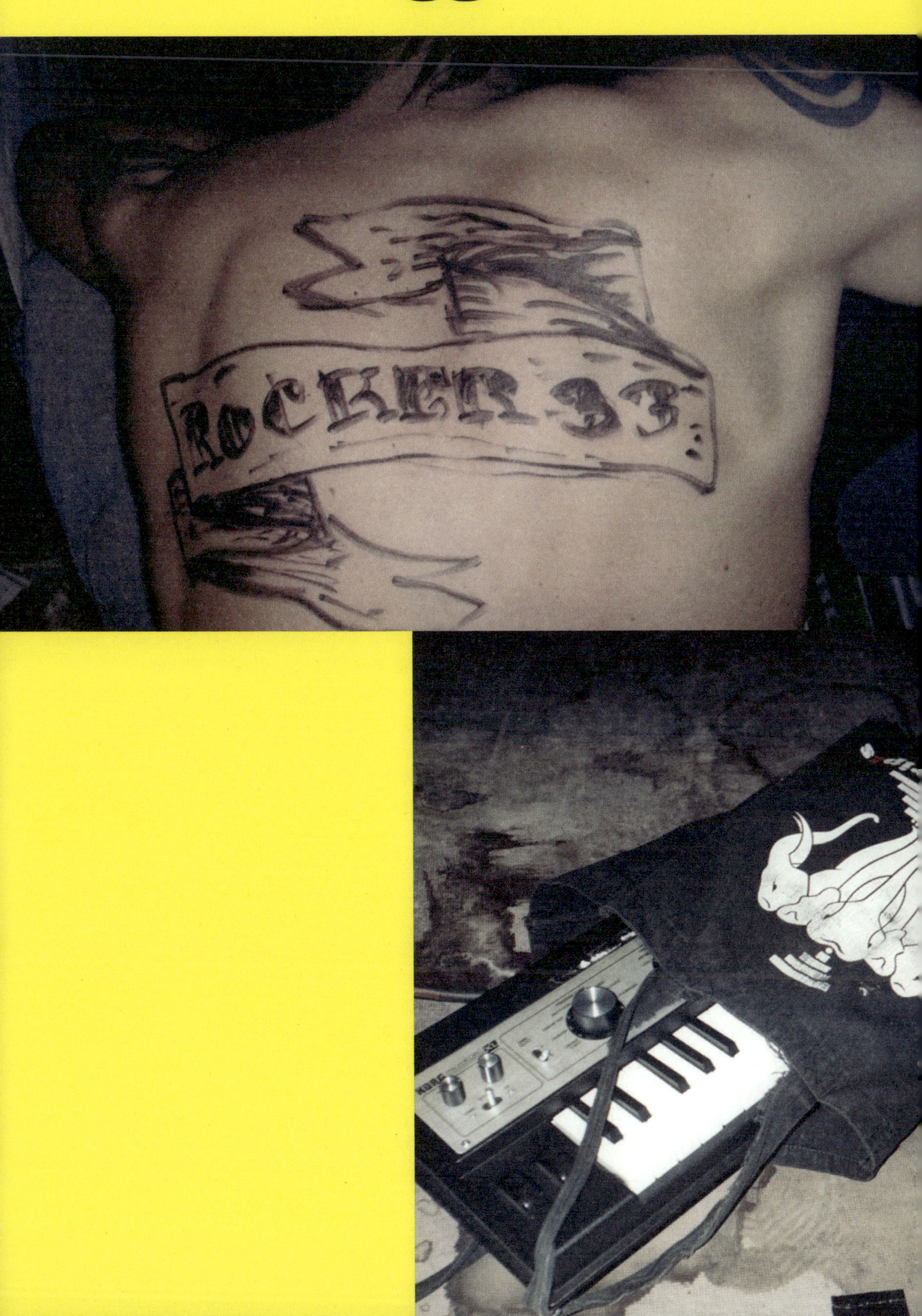

slayer oder boy george?

slayerrrr … die den mit marshmallows gefüllten boy george über einem spiess in der hölle braten.

auf welches konzert eines toten künstlers würdest du gerne gehen?

wesley willis. cab calloway. jimi hendrix. darby crash. d. boone. miles davis. john coltrane. muddy waters. john lee hooker. duke ellington. etta james. billy holiday. dean martin. frank sinatra. jim morrison. freddie mercury. ian curtis. keith moon. syd barret. brian jones. gg allin. john lennon. jaco pastorius. janis joplin. am liebsten alle auf einmal. Eine gigantische Zombie-Bigband, die von dem untoten Glen Miller dirigiert wird.

was kickt dich?

bass drums.

was nervt dich?

menschen, die erwarten, dass die dinge zu einem bestimmten zeitpunkt auf eine bestimmte weise sein müssen. na ja, nicht die leute selbst, aber ihre erwartungen sind scheiße. an alle anderen und an sich selbst. ähm, die kurze antwort lautet: erwartungen.

dr. jekyll oder mr. hyde?

es kann keinen ohne den anderen geben. das ist wie im richtigen Leben. kein vergnügen ohne schmerz. yin oder yang?

dein lieblingsgegenstand?

ich würde sagen, der große schwarze vibrator meiner freundin, aber sie würde mich wahrscheinlich umbringen, wenn sie das liest, also sage ich einfach: meine Freundin. aber warte, sie ist kein gegenstand … ich glaube, ich bin jetzt irgendwie in schwierigkeiten. ich finde, dass „lieblingsgegenstand" ein oxymoron ist. ein liebling ist nicht materiell.

noch was?

lass durch deine fehlende lebensplanung und deine erwartungen an das leben nicht zu, dass du unflexibel wirst und dadurch nicht mehr zur richtigen zeit am richtigen ort sein kannst. du musst dir immer eine entspannte haltung bewahren. denn das leben ist ein großes abenteuer!

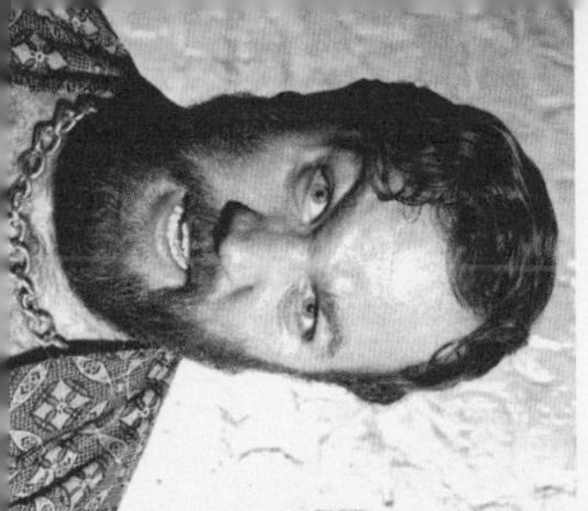

slayer or boy george?

slayerrrr … roasting boy george on a spit in hell stuffed with marshmallows.

on which concert of a dead artist would you like to go to?

wesley willis. cab calloway. jimi hendrix. darby crash. d. boone. miles davis. john coltrane. muddy waters. john lee hooker. duke ellington. etta james. billy holiday. dean martin. frank sinatra. jim morrison. freddie mercury. ian curtis. keith moon. syd barret. brian jones. gg allin. john lennon. jaco pastorius. janis joplin. preferably all at once. a gigantic zombie big band, conducted by an undead glen miller.

what kicks?

bass drums.

what sucks?

people who expect things to be a certain way at a certain time. well, not the people themselve. but their expectations suck. for everyone else as well as themselves. umm, the short answer: expectations.

dr. jekyll or mr. hyde?

you can't have one without the other. it's like real life. no pleasure no pain. yin or yang?

your love item?

i'd say my girlfriend's big black love vibrator, but she'd probably kill me if she read that, so i'll just say my girlfriend. but wait, she's not an item … i think i'm in trouble either way now. i think „love item" is an oxymoron. love is not material.

anything else?

allow your lack of planning and lack of expectations and the elasticity of your own life will put you in the right place at the right time. then all you have to do is to maintain the right state of mind. then: life is an amazing adventure!

CLOCKWISE:
ALEXANDER HACKE, DIGITALISM, ACID PAULI, ZOOT WOMAN,
WHITEST BOY ALIVE, SNAX, THOMILLA & MICHI BECK

KODAK 160NC
46
KODAK 160

54
KODAK 160NC-2
55
KO

51
KODAK 160NC
52

9 Volt
Batteries
NU
GROOVE

CLOCKWISE:
SASCHA HÉRISSON, ROBERT STADLOBER, ROCK KRAUS, SASCHA FUNKE,
OPTIMO, METRO AREA, TIEFSCHWARZ

PRO
VIDING
ART

NOT
SERVICE

JAHCOOZI
nutella
FILA
TOUR DE SUISSE
nutella
nutella
Kappa

THE BLOODY BEETROOTS

DEAD
CRUISER

POLIZEI

D Me and Rock'n'Roll, oder die Nacht, die dich und uns verbrennt. Was genau geschieht in diesem einen Moment, in dem die Zeit stehenzubleiben scheint, in dem du alles um dich herum vergisst, Stille der Wand aus Geräuschen weicht, in dem nur du da bist, obwohl der Raum voller bebender Leiber ist, in dem dein Körper aufhört Leib zu sein und nur noch das Gefühl bleibt? Dein Verstand hat dich verlassen, du bist frei. Redundante Musik treibt den Blutdruck mit wummernden Tiefen in die Höhe. Der monotone Schlag der Zwei und Vier ersetzt deinen Herzschlag, hypnotische Klangsequenzen versetzen die Bebenden in einen transzendenten Zustand, aus dem sie erst viel später unter Einsatz mäandernder Frequenzen wieder erlöst werden. Es ist 04:00 Uhr morgens, die Luft ist zum Schneiden, Stroboskobblitze durchdringen den Raum und zeichnen im Bruchteil einer Sekunde eine fahle Silhouette auf die zuckenden Körper, frieren die Bewegung teils anmutig, teils entstellt im Raum der Vergänglichkeit ein. Der DJ ist Gott und Teufel zugleich, treibt dich weiter und weiter an, fordert dir deine letzte Kraft ab, verlängert die automatisierte Bewegung deiner Beine, Arme und Hüften um immer noch einen weiteren Pulsschlag.

Natürlich hat nicht jede Nacht die Qualität, den Verstand zu verlieren. Aber manche davon bleiben für immer in Erinnerung. Nach sehr vielen schlecht besuchten Abenden und höchstens passabel gefüllten Tanzflächen musste wieder eine gute Nacht her — für die Kasse und für die Moral. Wir baten Steff die Gebrüder Schwarz anzurufen, einer seiner wichtigsten Kontakte. Es hat geklappt. Tiefschwarz war gebucht, an einem Freitag Ende Juni. Wir wussten, dass das ein Selbstläufer werden würde. Deswegen haben wir auch eine Stunde früher als üblich geöffnet. Die Schlange an der Tür war gigantisch, bis in die Klett-Passage rein. Die Menschen kamen, strömten rein und feierten ausgelassen und wild. Und es kamen immer mehr. Selbst um 03:00 Uhr nachts war die Schlange vor der

Tür noch nicht absehbar. Weil es schon schön sommerlich warm war, haben wir für diesen Abend eine provisorische Bar in den Innenhof gezimmert, mehr ein Bretterverschlag, der wie eine Strandbude wackelig im eigens aufgeschütteten Sand stand. Alle verfügbaren Mitarbeiter standen an den drei Bars, räumten Gläser und Flaschen ab und befüllten die Kühlschränke neu. Trotzdem waren wir dem Ansturm nicht gewachsen. Jetzt musste jeder mithelfen: Freunde, Bekannte, Fremde. „Hier ist der Kühlschrank, Bier kostet 3 Euro, Wodka Bull 5 Euro, raus damit!". Erst gingen die Eiswürfel aus, dann Getränke, dann Gläser. Aber die Massen waren durstig. Wir schenkten Wodka-Bull in Sektgläsern aus. Die Leute kamen mit irgendwelchen abstrusen Behältern, wie Spielzeugeimer und leere Aschenbecher, die sie im Hof gefunden hatten: „Mach irgendwas rein, egal!" — „Jacky Fanta? 5 Euro bitte."

Als die Sonne aufging zerrten Steff und Christian das kleine DJ Pult in den Hof und zogen von irgendwo noch Strom. Sie spielten im Sand und die Leute liebten sie dafür. Die letzten Gäste gingen um 10:00 Uhr morgens. Das war zweifellos eine dieser Nächte, die sich ins kollektive Gedächtnis brannte.

E Me and rock'n'roll, or the night that burns you and us. What exactly happens in this one moment, when the time seems to freeze and you forget everything around you, the quietness gives way to noises in which only you are, even though the room is full of quivering bodies and in which you stop being body and only your feelings remain? Your mind has left you – you are free. Redundant music boosts blood pressure with thundering lows. The monotonous beat of the two and four replaces your heartbeat, hypnotic sound sequences put the blood pressure in a transcendent state, from which they are redeemed much later using meandering frequencies. It's four o'clock in the morning, the air is thick as fog, stroboscopic flashes penetrate the room and draw a pale silhouette on the twitching bodies in a fraction of a second, freezing the movement partly graceful, partly disfigured in the space of transience. The DJ is God and devil at the same time, pushing you on and on, demanding your last strength, extending the automated movement of your legs, arms and hips with yet another pulse.

Of course, not every night has the quality to make you lose your mind. But some of them are remembered forever. After a lot of poorly attended evenings and rarely filled dance floors there had to be a good night again — for the bank account and for the morale of the team. We asked Steff to call the Schwarz brothers, one of his most important contacts. It worked out. Tiefschwarz was booked on a Friday in late June. We knew that would be a home run. That's why we opened one hour earlier than usual. The line on the door was gigantic, right into the Klett passage. The people came, poured in and celebrated like crazy. And more and more came. Even at 03:00 clock at night, the queue at the door was not foreseeable. Because it was nice and warm in the summer, we made an improvised bar in the courtyard for this evening, more like a shed, which stood like a beach shack wobbly in the specially heaped sand. All available girls and boys from our personal rooster were placed at the three bars, cleared glasses and bottles and refilled the refrigerators. Nevertheless, we were not up to the onslaught. Now everyone had to help: friends, acquaintances, strangers. „Here's the fridge, beer costs 3 euros, vodka bull 5 euros, get on with it!". First the ice cubes ran out, then drinks, then glasses. But the masses were thirsty. We served vodka-bull in champagne glasses. People came in with some awkward containers, like toy buckets and empty ashtrays found in the yard: „Put something in, no matter!" — „Jacky Fanta? 5 euros please."

As the sun rose, Steff and Christian dragged the little DJ desk into the yard and pulled electricity from somewhere. They played in the sand and people loved them. The last guests left at 10:00 in the morning. This was undoubtedly one of those nights that got burned into the collective memory.

I'M NOT
CRAZY
ABOUT
MONEY
BUT I
LIKE
WHAT IT
CAN DO

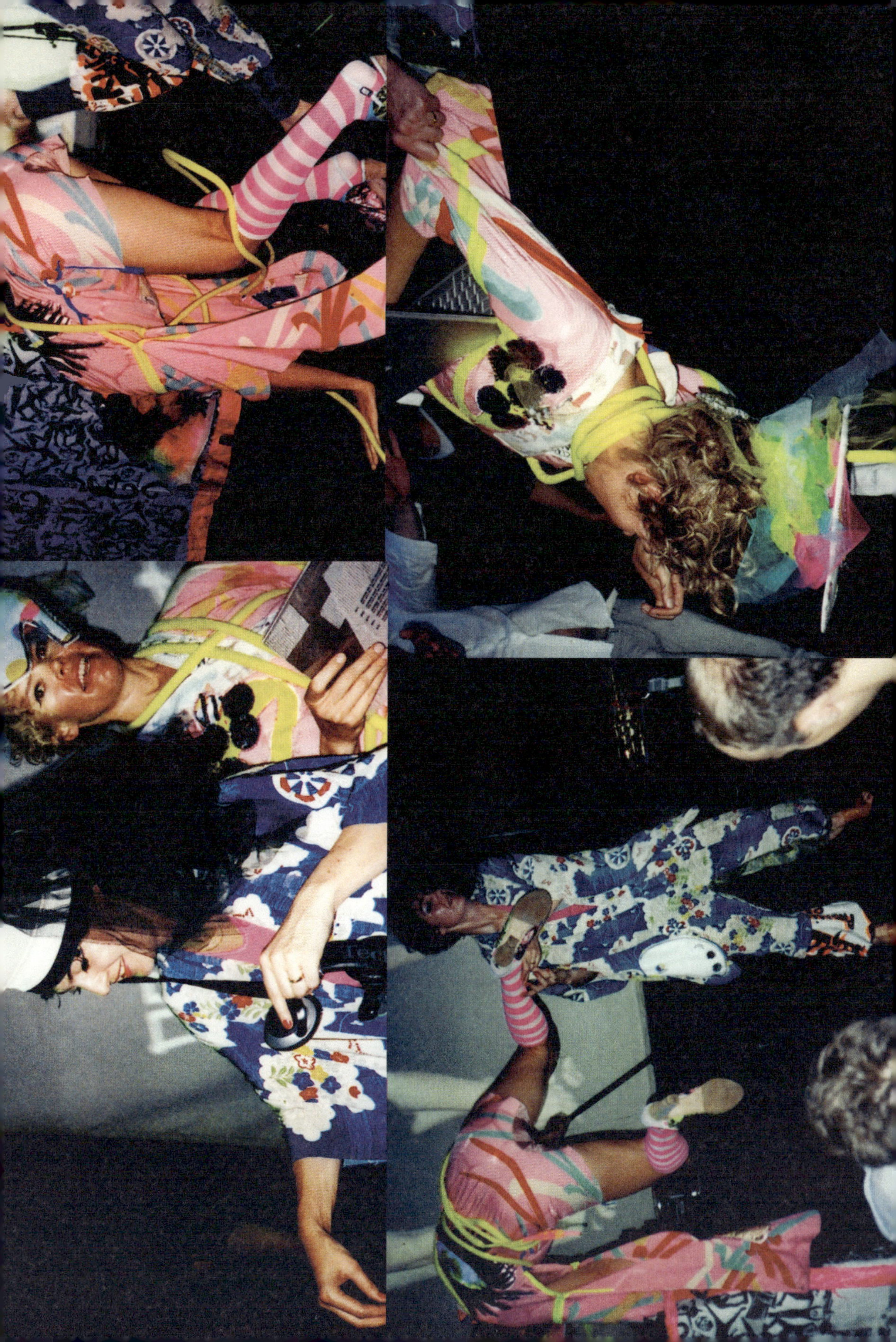

CLOCKWISE:
MODESELEKTOR, HOUSE OF FIX,
MEDIENGRUPPE TELEKOMMANDER
MR. OIZO, ROMAN FLÜGEL, SOULWAX

·CLOSER·

CLOCKWISE:
HEADMAN, JIMI TENOR, BOYS NOIZE, UFFIE,
ATA, JULIA HUMMER, STEVE KOTEY, FETISCH & TABI TABOO

NOW REPEAT
NOW REPEAT
NOW REPEAT

FISCHERSPOONER

REFLEX

COCK N BULL KID

LITTLE BOOTS

THE SAW IS THE LAW

MIGNON

„is this a garbage bag?"
„is that real blood?"

GONNA BURST INTO FLAME

D über das rocker haben wir schon nach dem fünften ton die kontrolle verloren. zur abwechslung hat die crowd uns auseinandergenommen. die bühne wurde konsequent leergeklaut. ein kleines debakel zwischen den peoples und buddy kam zustande: der kampf um die hüpfburg! sie wurde ihm entrissen und tanzte samt gebläse über den köpfen der leute. phono weinte—die hüpfburg ist sein ein und alles. der beamer und dessen halterung verloren die kraft und stürzten von der decke. der mensch darunter überlebte es. der beamer nicht.

ein gast lehnte sich über die bühne und nahm ein alkoholbad. buddy hob die whiskeyflasche und schüttete 2,5 liter aus. ein unglücklicher fehltritt kappte den strom. der cd-player fiel aus. es folgten pirouetten im nichts. phono überbrückte die stille minutenlang mit seiner stärke: waldorfmässiger ausdruckstanz! schliesslich hatte philipp die richtige stelle auf der cd gefunden … bon voyage pumpte pompös. auch das sperrige 70er jahre sofa, das mindestens 70kg wog, wurde vom publikum wider unseres willlens dreist an sich gerissen und bahnte sich auf händen getragen seinen weg durch den laden. der auftritt hat eine

**kontroverse diskussion in der band
entfacht: wer wird deutscher meister?**
E we lost control of the rocker after
the fifth note. the crowd tore us down.
the stage was consistently robbed.
a small debacle between the guests
and buddy came about: the fight
for the bouncy castle! it was snatched
from him and began wandering over
the peoples' heads. phono cried—
the bouncy castle was his one and
only. the projector and its bracket lost
their position and fell from the ceiling.
the guy under it survived. the projector
didn't.
  a guest leaned across the stage and
took an alcohol bath. buddy picked
up the whiskey bottle and poured at
least 2.5 liters over him. an unfortu-
nate misstep cut off the electricity. the
cd player went off. we had to improvise.
phono bridged the silence with
his strength for minutes: waldorf-like
expressive dance! finally, philipp
had found the right spot on the cd …
„bon voyage" pumped pompously. even
the bulky 70s sofa, which weighed at
least 70kg, was captured by the crowd
against our will and made its way
through the venue on those numerous
hands hands. the performance
has sparked a controversial and
controversial discussion in the band:
who will be german champion?

BUDDY (DEICHKIND)

1 ... 2 ...
prayer ...

togehter ...
let there be rock!

THORSTEN

DIRTY PRINCESS

EAST RIVER
ROCK FIGHT

OPEN LATE
THE GREEK MiSS
SEEKS
PROFFESSOR
CALL Now!!
262 3379

D Tag für Tag ging ins Land und in die Stadt — mehr aber noch die Nächte. Nach Abenden mit beinahe nicht zu bewältigendem Andrang folgten Abende nahezu ohne jegliche Besucher. Auf und ab, up and down. Hinzu kamen zahlreiche Auflagen von den Behörden und der Stadtverwaltung. Als temporäres Projekt wollte der Club nicht mehr wahrgenommen werden. Dafür aber als Betrieb mit den damit verbundenen Investitionen, die es aufzubringen galt. Ob in guten oder schlechten Zeiten. Mit Höhen und Tiefen. Kunst und Experimente und das ewige Trial-and-Error-Prinzip wurden ausgetauscht gegen Pragmatismus, Routine und einem Hauch Professionalität. Dann, nach Monaten und Jahren des Zitterns und Wackelns, nach personellen Veränderungen und inhaltlicher Manifestierung geriet das Schiff in unternehmerisch ruhigeres Fahrwasser. Was jedoch niemals ruhig bleiben sollte, waren die Nächte ...

War jedoch wenig los, wurde es zäh. Der Rocker 33 konnte verdammt groß sein. Und kalt. Wenig Gäste hieß schlechte Stimmung. Auch beim Personal, weil das Arbeiten öde wurde. Überflüssige Barkräfte schickten wir nach Hause. Nicht selten begannen Gäste aus Langeweile zu randalieren. Sie zertrümmerten unsere Toiletten und schlugen immer und immer wieder die Feuermelder ein. Jeder Fehlalarm bei der Feuerwehr kostete uns bis zu 1500 Euro, wenn der gesamte Löschzug anrücken musste. Gäste können Arschlöcher sein. Sie beschmieren das gesamte Gebäude von außen und innen, geistern und demolieren durch die Gänge, stehlen Getränke, öffnen ihren Freunden die Fluchtwege nach außen, um keinen Eintritt zahlen zu müssen.

Sie nörgeln und beschweren sich. Ab und zu prügeln sie sich. Manchmal haben wir unsere Gäste gehasst.

E Days and days went passing by — but even more the nights. Evenings with almost unmanageable rushes were followed by evenings with almost no visitors. Up and down and back again. In addition, numerous editions of the authorities and the city administration. The club could no longer be ignored as a temporary project. It was considered as a business with the associated investments. Whether in good or bad times. With highs and lows. Art and experiments and the eternal trial-and-error principle were exchanged for pragmatism, routine and a touch of professionalism. Then, after months and years of trembling and shaking, after personnel changes and content manifestation, the ship came into entrepreneurially calmer waters. But what should never be quiet was the nights.

It was tough going. The venue could be damn big. And cold. Few guests meant bad vibes. Also with the staff, because working was boring. Superfluous bar staff were sent home. Not seldomly, guests began to riot out of boredom. They smashed our toilets and hit the fire alarms over and over again. Each false alarm at the fire department could cost us up to 1500 euros. Guests can be assholes. They spray tag the entire building from outside and inside, ghosting and demolishing through the corridors, stealing drinks, opening the escape routes to their friends to avoid having to pay admission. They nag and complain. Now and then they beat each other up. Sometimes we hated our guests.

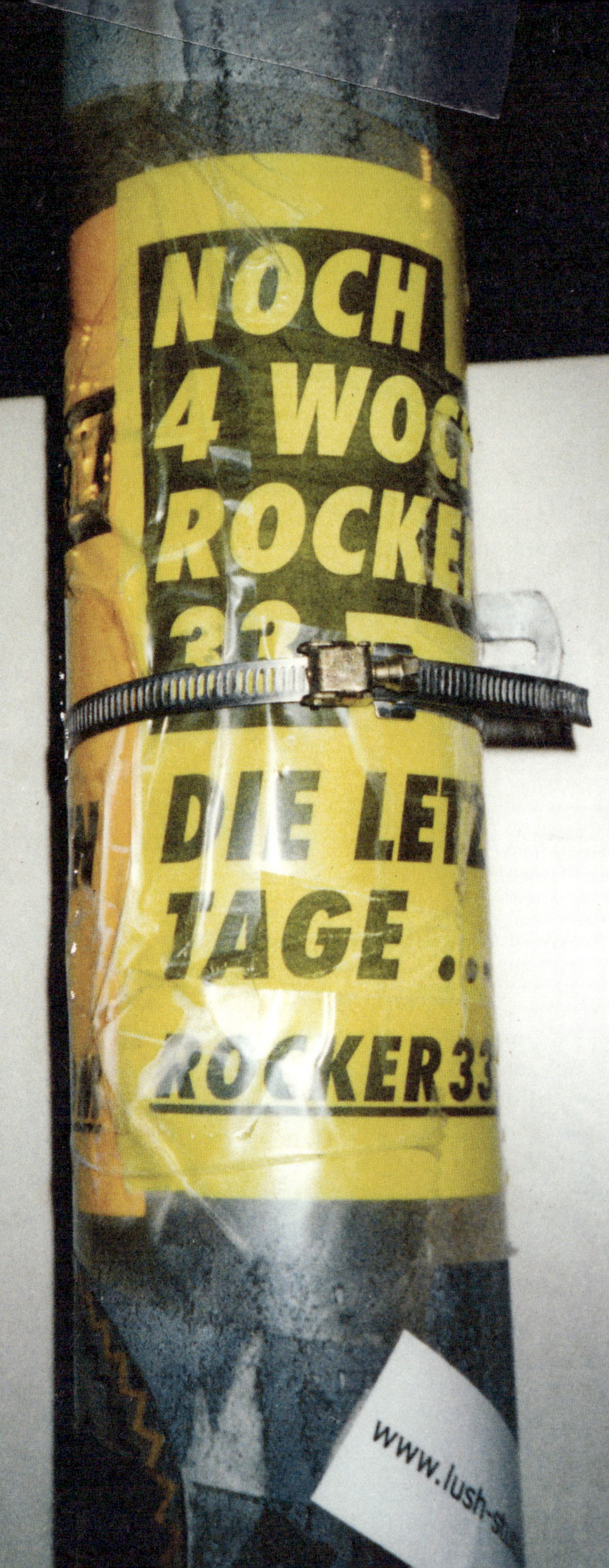

NOCH
4 WOC
ROCKE
33
DIE LETZ
TAGE...
ROCKER33
www.lush-st

Are you experienced?

Hey! Your slot begins in 5 minutes.
I wear my sunglasses at night.

I´m so glad I brought my towel.
When will I ... will I be famous?

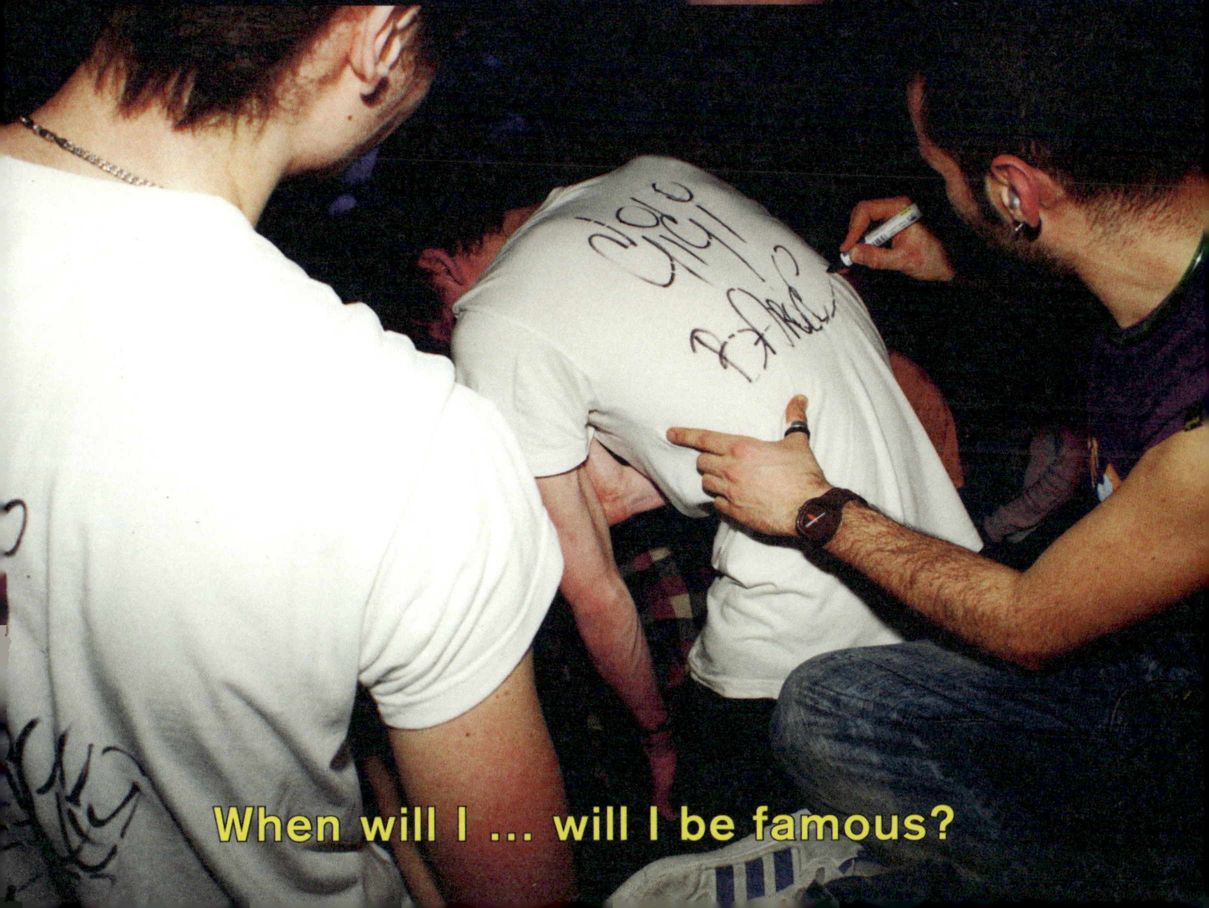

SKID ROW
MASTER OF PUPPETS
SAXON
SEPULTU

MISS KITTIN

DJ FRICTION

ZOMBIE DISCO
SQUAD

VOGUE
1990

CHICKS ON SPEED

LOVE
FIX YOUR TARGET
LET YOUR SPIRIT GROW
DO NOT BETRAY YOUR FRIEND
SAVE NATURE
SHARE
ON
OTHERS
DO NOT
MURDER
SHARE
BE TEMPERATE
WORK HARD
DO NOT STEAL
AVOID VIOLENCE
PROTECT YOURSELF AND OTHERS
SEEK TRUTH
CO
BE POLITE
FULFILL YOUR OBLIGATIONS
DO NOT DIE
COME TOGETHER
CLEAN YOUR HEART
HONOR AND HELP YOUR PARENTS
BE PEACEFUL
SET A GOOD EXAMPLE
TREAT EVERYONE
ENJOY
LET IT HAPPEN
DON'T

SUMMER TIME

TIME TO SIT BACK AND UNWIND

DJ JAZZY JEFF

CHRISTIAN

DAVE

D The beauty of trash. Und was davon übrig bleibt. Angezogen von dunklen, düsteren Momenten, immer in sich ruhend, in der Stille, kurz vor dem Ausbruch, der Explosion. Im Lärm der Stille finden sich schimmernde Sakrale der Einsamkeit und des Glücks. Immer wieder. Aber nicht immer. Was als Tempel der Egomanie entstand, verselbständigte sich, erlebte Höhen und Tiefe, zerbrach in seine Bestandteile, um sich wieder aus der eigene Asche zu erheben. Give me faith. Warum sich alles zuerst erschüttern muss, bevor es sich bewegt, liegt in der Natur der Dinge. Komm mit. Dorthin, wo du dir selbst begegnen sollst.

Glamour ist so lange aufregend, bis es zur Routine wird. Wenn einer von uns an einem Abend „Dienst" hatte, bedeutet dies eine komplizierte Abfolge einstudierter Abläufe: Bevor Personal und Gäste kamen, liefen wir durch die langen Bürospangen des Gebäudes rund um den Innenhof und öffneten einige Räume mit einem Dietrich-artigen Schlüssel. Die 20 Lampen, die den Hof aus Ästhetik- und Sicherheitsgründen illuminieren sollten, steckten wir von Hand ein. Alle einzeln. Dann das Übliche: Wechselgeld vorbereiten, Barbestände prüfen, Technikcheck. Personal begrüßen und einweisen. Kassen mit Wechselgeld und Stempel bestücken. Und hoffen, dass bald und vor allem viele Gäste kamen. Waren es viele, war die Nacht schnell vorbei: Überquellende Geldbeutel abschöpfen, DJs bespaßen, Personal unterstützen, notfalls ausgegangene Getränke organisieren. Morgens um 06:00 Uhr ging das Putzlicht an, dann musste das Personal Klarschiff machen, die Bar wieder bestücken, wir bezahlten die Mitarbeiter, zählten die Einnahmen, machten alle Hoflichter wieder aus. Abschließen. Nicht selten wurde es 09:00 Uhr morgens bis sich der eigene Haustürschlüssel im Schloss drehte.

Wir beschlossen viel. Meist nach endlosen Diskussionen. Oft hielten wir uns an das Vereinbarte. Aber nicht immer. Wir gingen einen Schritt nach vorn — dann wieder zwei zurück. Wir redeten und redeten, hatten große Ideen und kleine Einfälle. Die meisten Gedanken verloren sich im Tagesgeschäft. Es war uns allen klar, dass dieses labile Konstrukt aus Ego und Nachtleben nicht ewig Bestand haben würde. Wir

wussten, dass der Moment irgendwann vorbei
sein würde. Aber noch nicht jetzt. Nicht heute Nacht!

E The beauty of trash. And what is left of it. Attracted by dark, gloomy moments, always at rest, in the silence, just before the outbreak, the explosion. In the noise of silence there are shimmering sacral solitudes and happiness. Again and again. But not always. What arose as a temple of egomania, became independent, experienced heights and depths, broke into its components, to rise again from its own ashes. Give me faith. Why everything must first get torn down before it moves comes quite natural. Come along with us. Where you shall meet yourself.

Glamour is exciting until it becomes routine. If one of us was in charge at night, it would mean a complicated sequence of rehearsed procedures: before staff and guests arrived we walked through the long office clasps of the building around the courtyard and opened some rooms with a picklock. All of the 20 lamps that should illuminate the courtyard for aesthetic and safety reasons had to be switched on by hand. Then the usual stuff: prepare change, bar inventory, technical check. Welcoming and instructing the staff. Cash registers with change and stamp equipment. And hoping that a lot of guests will come soon. If there were a lot, the night was quickly over: skimming overflowing purses, entertaining the DJs, supporting staff, if necessary organize drinks that went off. In the morning at 06:00 o'clock, the cleaning light went on. Then the staff had to clean up the mess, equip the bar again. The employees were paid on the spot, the revenue was counted, all yard lights turned off again. Locking everything. Not seldomly, it was 09:00 clock in the morning when your own key turned in the door of your flat.

We decided a lot. Mostly after endless discussions. Often we adhered to the agreed. But not always. We took a step forward — then two steps back. We talked and talked, had great ideas and little incidences. Most of our notions got lost in daily business. It was clear to all of us that this fragile construct of ego and nightlife would not last forever. We knew that the moment would be over at some point. But not now. Not tonight!

EAT
MORE

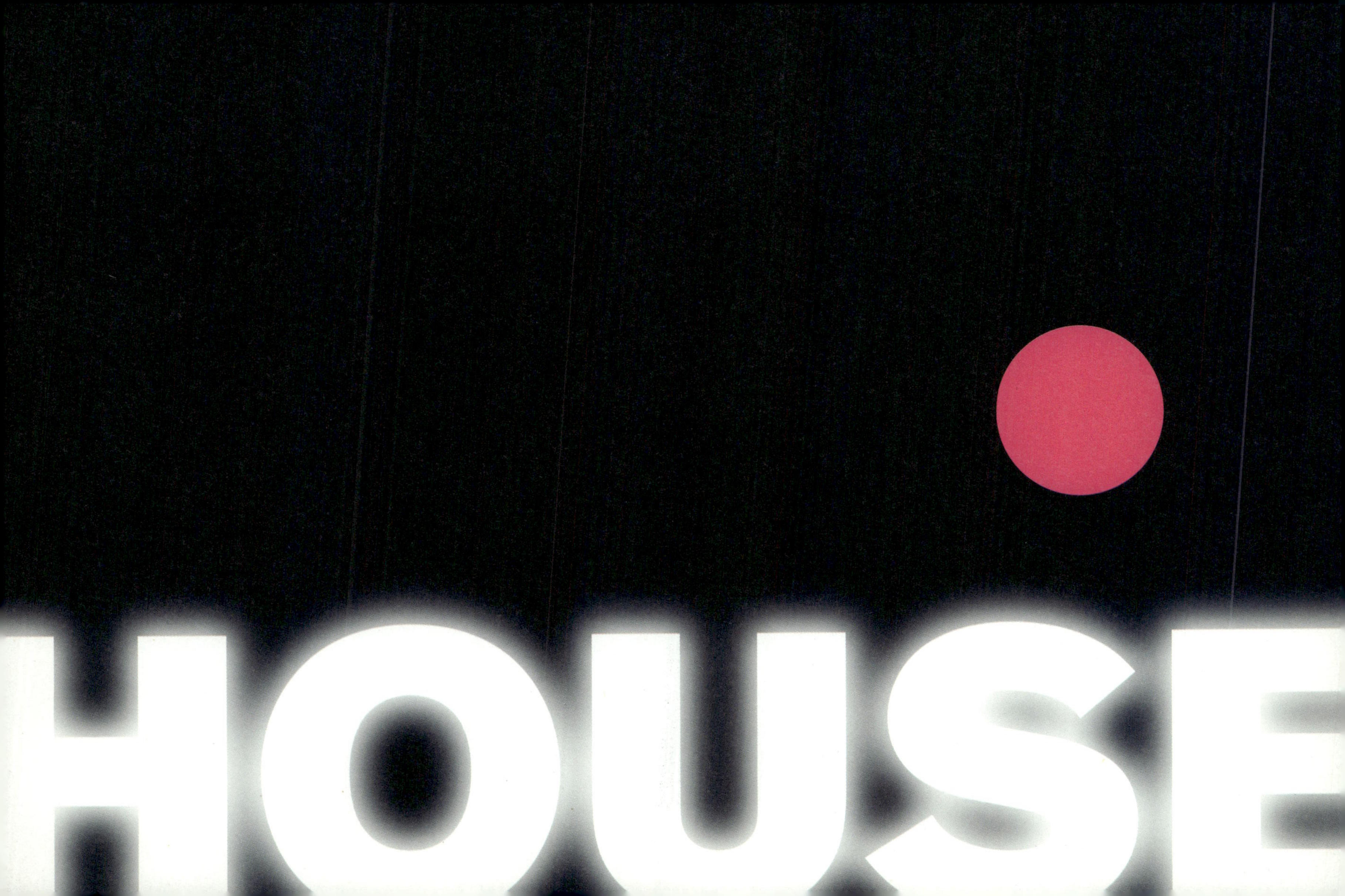
HOUSE

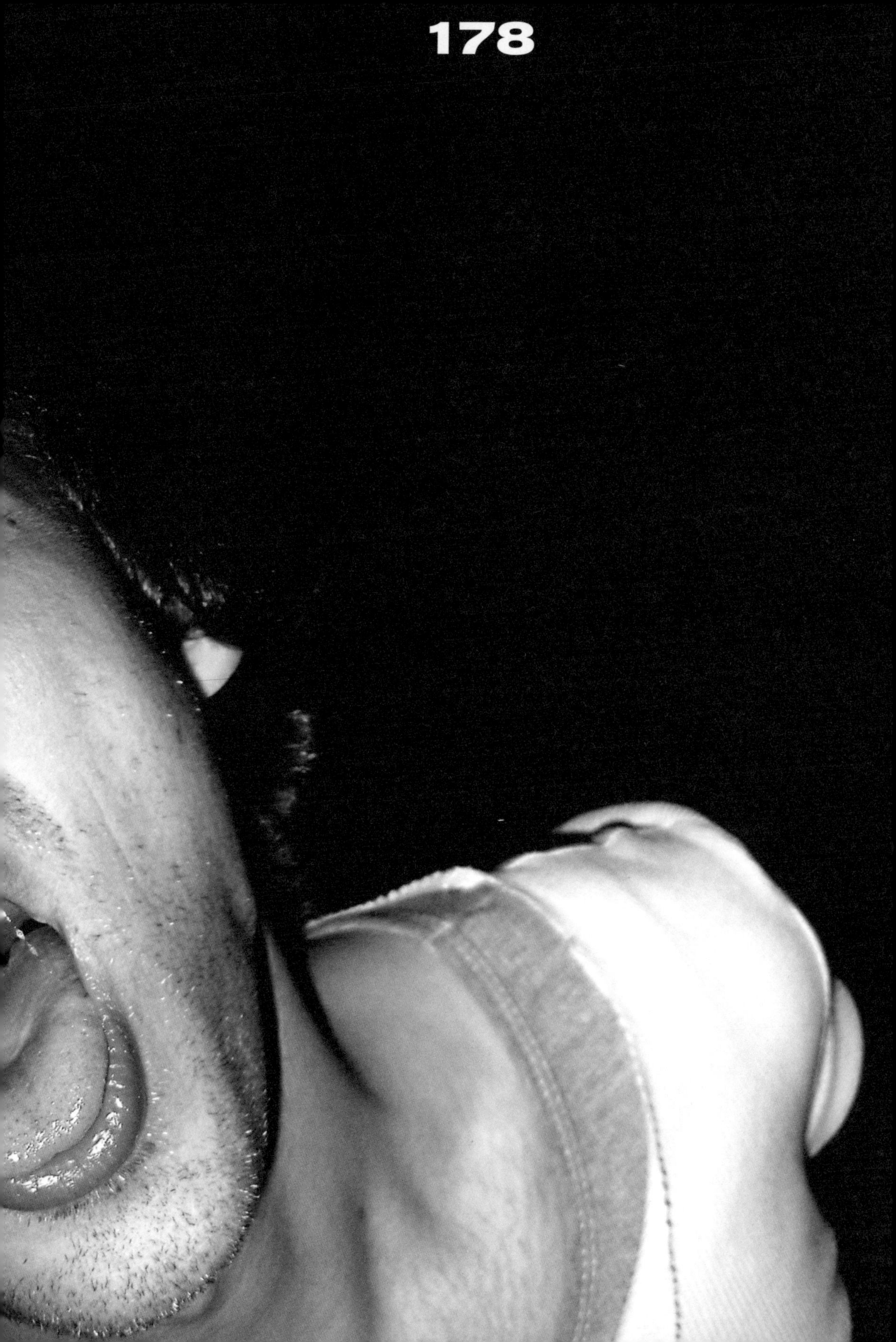

BORN TO BE
WILD

KEEP SAFE AND

STAY POSITIVE

FELIX DA HOUSECAT

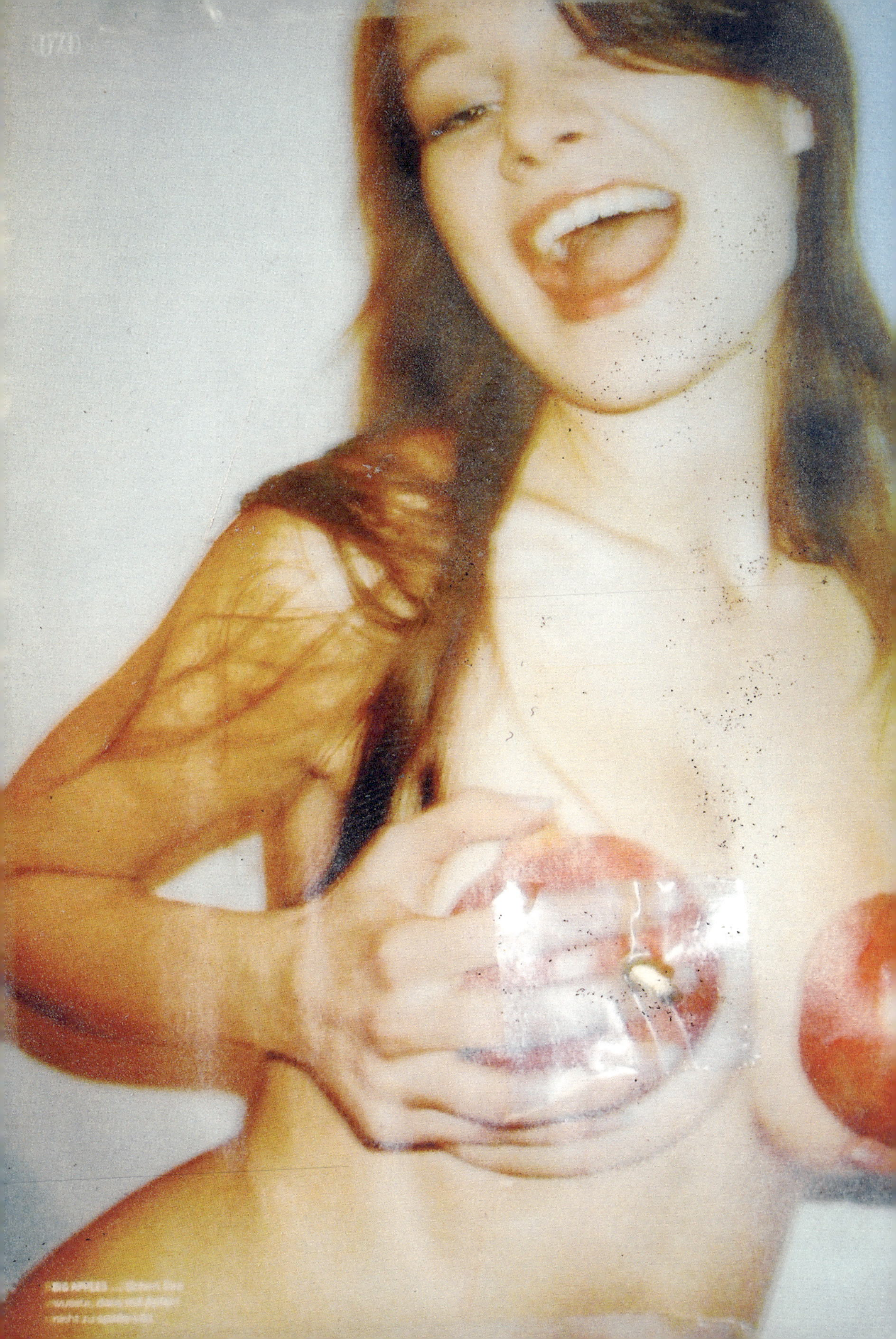

CRACK

A SMILE FOR ME

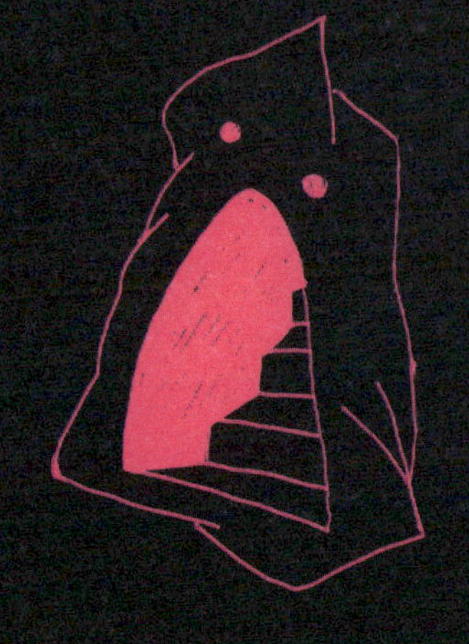

MINUTE NOW
NOT MY STYLE SO HURRY UP ANY
TE NOW CAUSE IT'S

RUN THINK FAST IT WILL CATCH UP WITH YOU ANY MIN

BOSCH
THE JETSET

IF I GAVE YOU A PARTY I WOULD COME

cassette
cassette
cassette
cassette
cassette
casset
casse
cass
cass
cass
PUNKS
JUMP UP

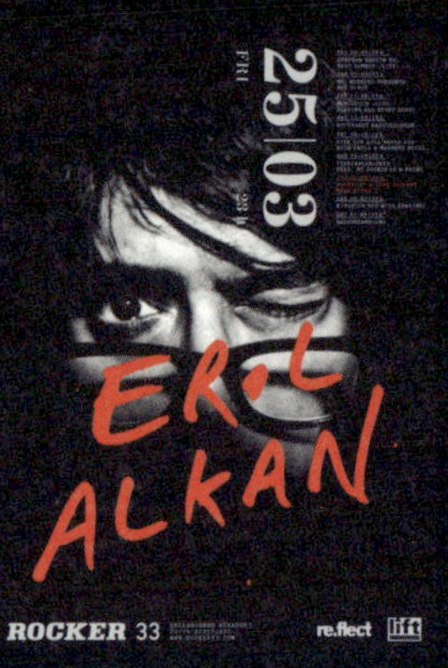
FRI
25|03
ERoL
ALKAN
ROCKER 33
re.flect lift

Corona Extra
SAT
16|04
DJ
JAZZY
JEFF
*SUPPORT: DJ EMILIO
ROCKER 33
WeSC PRINZ

21.09.
/
23:00
SOUL
CLAP
WOLF + LAMB
BOSTON
ROCKER 33

04 07
FRI
MR. SUPER DISCOUNT FROM PARIS
ETIENNE
DE CRECY
* SUPPORT BY ALEXANDER MAIER (MOOD MUSIC)
VISUALS BY VJ R:A:U:L:
ROCKER 33

THEMENABEND
WHITE MEETS BLACK
FRI
24|08
23 h
BLACK
GRASS
LIVE
SUPPORT: GORDON 3000
ROCKER 33

DILLON
WED
14|12
20 h
ROCKER 33

SAT
02|10
DER DRITTE RAUM
ROCKER 33 partysan

19.10.
/
23:00
AKA
AKA
FEAT. THALSTROEM
SUPPORT
ALEXANDER MAIER
ROCKER 33 PRINZ

12.10.
/
23:00
BITCH
SUPPORT
RAPHAEL
DINCSOY
ROCKER 33

physical
SAT
25|10
DJT
ROCKER 33

SAT
03|09
23 h
PERMANENT
VACATION
NIGHT
BOSTRO PESOPEO
MUALLEM
FLORIAN EHING
CHRISTIAN SCHILLER
ROCKER 33

FRI
03
/
08
23 h
FLASHDANCE!
- 80IES - POP - NEW WAVE -
ROCKER 33

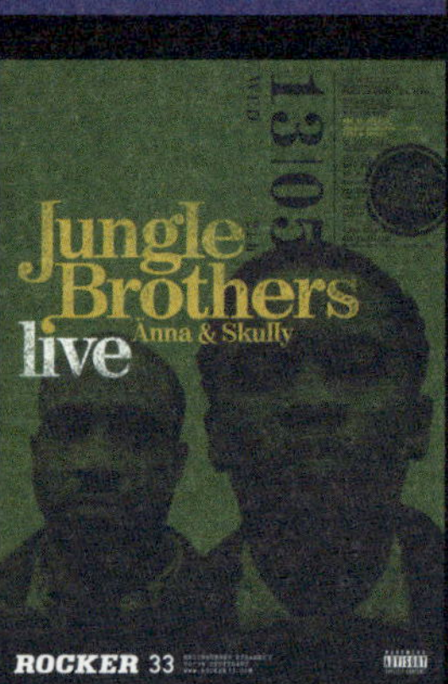
WED
13|05
Jungle
Brothers
live
Anna & Skully
ROCKER 33

05 09
FRI
23 h
FUMAKILLA
LABELNIGHT - PART II
WOODY
AND
JONA
SUPPORT: JURICAN (GIGOLO RECORDS)
ROCKER 33

30.
03.
/
23
00
STIMM
ING
LIVE
HAMBURG
SUPPORT ALEXANDER
MAIER
CAMPING
ROCKER 33

15 07
MAD DECENT
SOUND PELLEGRINO
LONDON
L-VIS
1990
SUPPORT BY
FRESH JUICE & DENSON
ROCKER 33

10|07
SAT
DAVE CLARKE UK
ALEXANDER MAIER
VISUALS BY
FRISCHVERGIFTUNG
ROCKER 33

14.09. / 23:00
PANTHA DU PRINCE
DIAL RECORDS
SUPPORT:
ALEXANDER MAIER
ROCKER 33

FRI
19 10
23 h
TERMINAL M
ELECTRIC AVENUE
MONIKA KRUSE
SUPPORT: BRENDAN HAAR
ROCKER 33
lift

MR WEEKEND PRESENTS
FEADZ
A.DENSON & BUSY ICER
+ SUPER SUPER
SA 16.01.10
ROCKER 33
re.flect

23|02
SAT
V
CHLOÉ
KILL THE DJ
PARIS
SUPPORT
BY
CHRISTIAN
SCHILLER
ROCKER 33

14 12
FRI
DIG ITALISM
LIVE
SUPPORT: CAJUAN (HH), CHRISTIAN SCHILLER
ROCKER 33
Motor FM
PRINZ

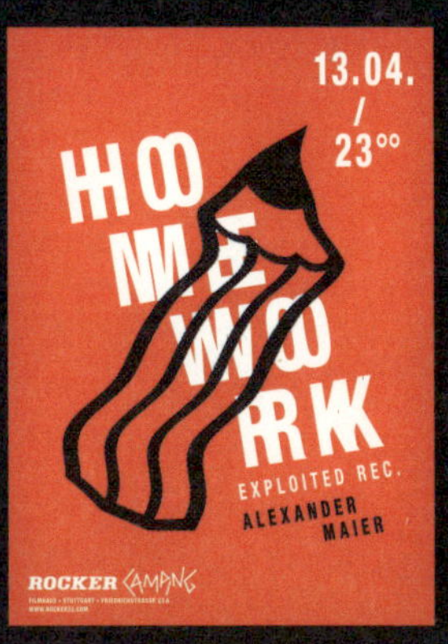

13.04. / 23:00
HOMEWORK
EXPLOITED REC.
ALEXANDER
MAIER
ROCKER CAMPING

border community
27|03
FRI
James Holden
ROCKER 33

16 11
FRI
BOYS NOIZE
BOYSNOIZE REC.
SUPPORT: JOHN DISCO
VISUALS: VJ SMIG
ROCKER 33
PRINZ

sunshine live
05.04. / 23:00
LEXY K-PAUL
ALEXANDER MAIER LIVE
ROCKER CAMPING

29 02
FRI
ÂME
(INNERVISIONS)
SUPPORT: CHRISTIAN SCHILLER
VISUALS: VJ REVOLIZER
ROCKER 33

12 12
FRI
MODE SELEKTOR
LIVE PFADFINDEREI
VISUALS BY
SUPPORT: CHRISTIAN SCHILLER
ROCKER 33

03|11
SAT
GIGOLO RECORDS
van MIJK DIJK
SUPPORT: ALL-STAR / VISUALS: VJ RIA(VJ)
ROCKER 33

25 04
FRI
IVAN SMAGGHE
KILL THE DJ
PARIS
CHRISTIAN SCHILLER
VJ REVOLIZER
ROCKER 33

11.05. / 23:00
keinemusik
LABELNIGHT
ADAM PORT · RAMPA · &ME
ROCKER CAMPING

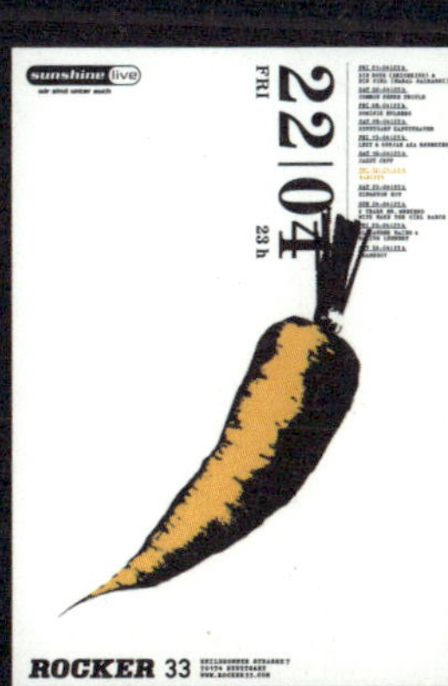

sunshine live
wir sind unter euch
22|04
FRI
23 h
ROCKER 33

11 | 11
FRI
23 h
ROCKER 33

28 | 12
FRI
23 h
DESSOUS BEST SECRET TOUR
WITH
PHONIQUE CLE
& VINCENZO
ROCKER 33

07 | 11
FRI
A PART OF
GANG STARR
SUPPORT BY EMILIO
DJ Premier
ROCKER 33

28 | 06
SAT
ALTER
EGO LIVE
KLANG ELEKTRONIK
SUPPORT: CHRISTIAN SCHILLER
VISUALS: FIDE AND RATHOFF
ROCKER 33

10 | 04
FRI
23 h
ONGAKU, COCOON.NET
JOHANNES
HEIL
- LIVE -
JÜRGEN KIRSCH & MICHA KLANG
(GLÜCKSKIND)
ROCKER 33   GLÜCKSKIND

19.05.
/
23:00
MONIKA
KRUSE
TERMINAL M
ADA
PAMPA AREAL
ROCKER CAMPING
sunshine

31 | 05
SAT
Flashdance
WE PLAY 80s POP ++ NEW WAVE ++ MODERN DANCE
ROCKER 33

08.06.
/
23:00
MANIK
NEW YORK
AND
LAURA
JONES
CHRISTIAN SCHILLER
ROCKER 33

06 | 03
THU
GALLUZZI
ANDRE
ROCKER 33   SOUTHERN COMFORT

25 | 01
FRI
23 h
SWAYZAK
!K7 RECORDS / BERLIN
SUPPORT: ALEXANDER MAIER
VISUALS BY VJ SMIG
LIVE
ROCKER 33

19 | 09
MARAL
SALMASSI
ZERO CASH LIVE
SUPPORT: KRM
ROCKER 33

lift
27.04.
/
23:00
ALBUM RELEASE TOUR
TERRA
NO
VA
ROCKER CAMPING

06 | 12
THU
NEW JUDAS
NEW YOUNG PONY CLUB LIVE
DAVID GILMOUR GIRLS LIVE
DJ BOBMO
ROCKER 33

30 | 09
FRI
LIVE
AT
ROBE
JOHNS
ROCKER 33

27 | 07
FRI
23 h
ACID
MARIA
FEMALE PRESSURE, SALON MIEZI / BERLIN
SUPPORT: BRENDAN HAAR (MELBOURNE)
ROCKER 33

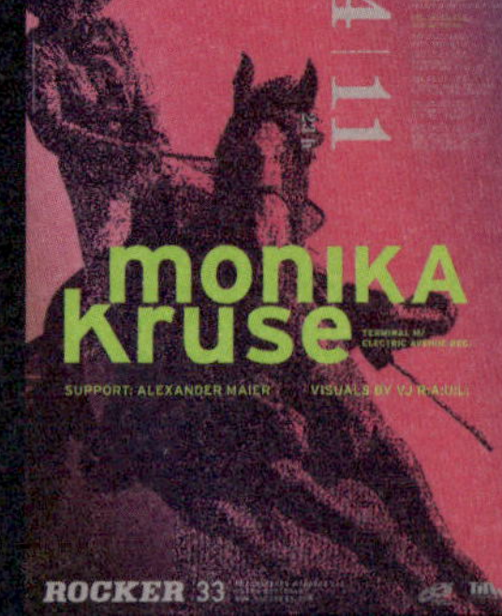
14 | 11
FRI
monika
kruse
ELECTRIC KINGDOM REC.
SUPPORT: ALEXANDER MAIER   VISUALS BY VJ MAIEL
ROCKER 33

M.A.N.D.Y.
PHILIPP
26 09
FRI
23 h
ROCKER 33

Stuttgarter Hofbräu
FRI
28 / 09
23 h
Ed Banger Rec. Paris
+ DJ Feadz
LIVE
ROCKER 33
MotorFM

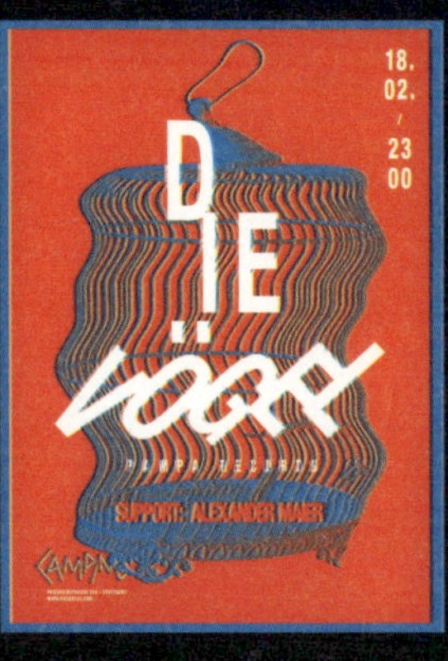
DIE VOGEL
18. 02. / 23 00
SUPPORT: ALEXANDER MAIER
CAMPING

14 09 FRI
DFA
23 h
SHIT ROBOT
SUPPORT: MANUEL BÜRGER
ROCKER 33

29 07 FRI
23 h
MARKUS LANGE &
(DIM MAK / DUSTED DECKS)
DJANE VANILLA
(SIMMA / DUSTED DECKS)
OSTBLOCK SCHLAMPEN
SUPPORT BY
MISS EVOICE &
DAS CARMA
ROCKER 33

FRI
20 / 07
23 h
JUSTUS KÖHNCKE
KOMPAKT
SUPPORT: ALEXANDER MAIER
(BUZZIN' FLY, 26TH CENTURY)
ROCKER 33

ROCKER 33 PRESENTS
02. 03. / 23 00
DIRT CREW (NIGHT)
DIRT CREW s
ELEF s
ALEXANDER MAIER s
CAMPING

FRI
17 / 08
23 h
DIALEKT E.V. PRÄSENTIERT
EXZESS & KONTROLLE
DEEP DARK & DIRTY MIT
MOUNT SIMS
INT. GIGOLO REC. LOS ANGELES
SUPPORT: THE CLUBKID, VISUALS: VJ MINUS
ROCKER 33

SAT
19 / 03
23 h
TURN TABLE ROCKER
33 rpm
ROCKER 33
PiG PRINZ

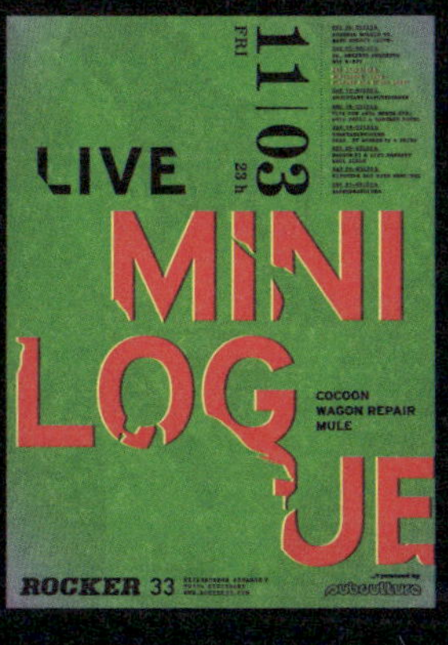
FRI
11 / 03
23 h
LIVE
MINILOGUE
COCOON
WAGON REPAIR
MULE
ROCKER 33

FRI
20 / 03
Chloé
KILL THE DJ / KITSUNÉ
ATA
ROBERT JOHNSON
SUPPORT:
CHRISTIAN SCHILLER
ROCKER 33
lift

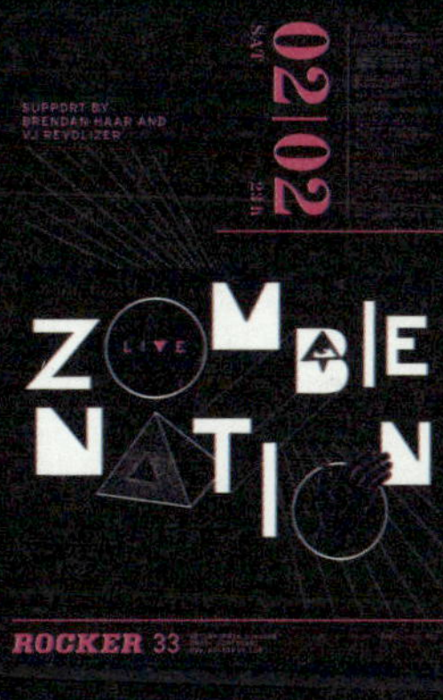
SAT
02 / 02
23 h
SUPPORT BY:
BRENDAN HAAR AND
VJ REVOLIZER
ZOMBIE NATION
LIVE
ROCKER 33

border community
FRI
17 / 10
20 h
NATHAN FAKE
LIVE
ROCKER 33

FRI
23 / 12
23 h
BORIS DLUGOSCH
FOUR ARTISTS HAMBURG
ROCKER 33

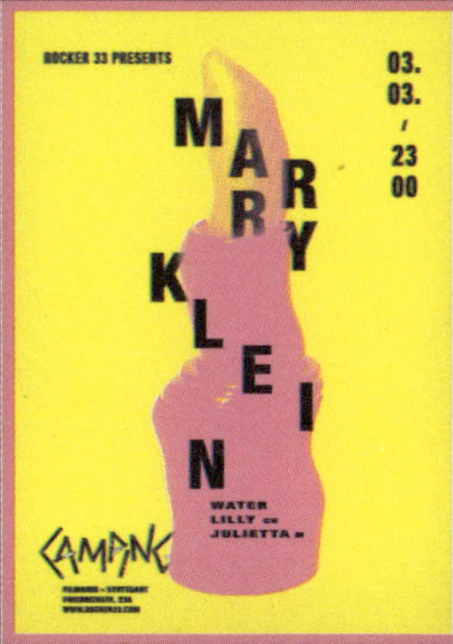
ROCKER 33 PRESENTS
03. 03. / 23 00
MARY KLEIN
WATER
LILLY OR
JULIETTA or
CAMPING

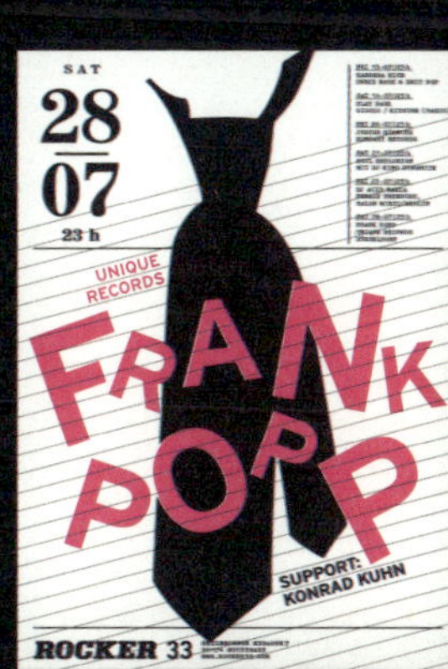
SAT
28 / 07
23 h
UNIQUE RECORDS
FRANK POPP
SUPPORT:
KONRAD KUHN
ROCKER 33

OPTIMO
22.07 23:00 FRIDAY
rocker 33 presents
jahcoozi
KittyYo/Berlin
live
Electronic Beats
with Ragga, Dancehall
& Hip Hop
22.10.
SA, 23.00 Uhr
with support by
kleinkariert
Rocker33
Heilbronner Str. 7
www.rocker33.com
COMPUTER GAMES
Hometrainer
rocker 33, heilbronner strasse 7, am bahnhof, stgt
DOXA RECORDS
ROCKER 33
& ELETTRO
BESTIA
present
SAT.
05.11
23.00 UHR
MENTAL GROOVE
Water
lilly
HARTCHEF
audio werner
hr schneider
erk richter
toc Electric - Krise
ali & der knart
ROCKER 33.com
HEILBR

Lee
★ ROCKER 33 PRESENTS ★
DEICH
KIND
music ★ super ★ danc
5.11.0
ss 21.

from Cologne
SCHAEBEN
& VOSS
FIRM / KOMPAKT RECORDS
LIVE!
SAT 02-JUL
23.00
AT ROCKER 33
HEILBRONNER STR. 7 GEGENUBER HBF

ROCKER PRESENTS
ROCKER
KIKI
Bpitch Control, Berlin
DANNY WANG
KAOS
K7! Records, Berlin
Fr, 14.Okt
www.rocker33.com
heilbronner str. 7
stuttgart

AUFDICKASSE ENTERTAINMENT
PRESENTS
SPIRITU DEL SUR
DIABLO DEL NORTE
LECKO
BERSERKO
VS
RED
ROCKET
LB
RR
ROCKER33
2005

ultimate
entertainment
ROCKER 33 PRÄSENT
TOM
BOY
WWW.GOMMA.DE
rocke
heilbronner
am bahnho
ROCKER 33
STR. 7
30
FAKE live! TNT Jackson (Wien)
THE RAPPER SA 15. OKT 23.00
ELECTRO ★ RAP ★ GALORE
SUPPORT BY DANIEL VARGA
WWW.ROCKER33.COM
Captain Comatose
PLAYHOUSE RECORDS
LIVE IN CONCERT!

live on
the wheel
of steel!!!
crazy
bastards
DJ
HUMPTYS PROUDLY PRESENTS
21ST CENTURY FIX
THE HOUSE OF FIX
THE HOUSE OF FIX
WITH SUPPORT BY
JESUS RODRIGUEZ & ACHIM KOSTRON
SATURDAY
28TH JANUARY
25. Juni 2005 * 23.00
* DANCE MODERN *
HEADMAN
FINE REC ★ RELISH ★ GOMMA
SA 11. JUNI
PLAYTIME 23.00

LIFE
SUCCESS
PAIN
REFLEX
LOVE
ICON
TRASH
33

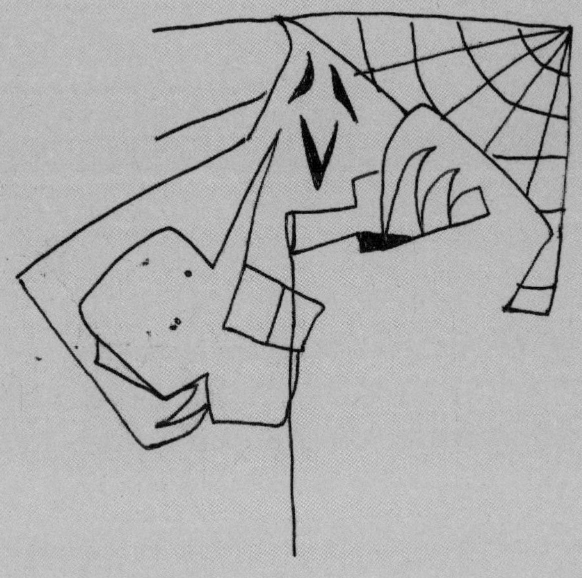

The Core
Pejo Babic
Steff Deininger
Thorsten Neumann
Christian Schiller
Matthias Straub

The Crew
David Spaeth
Julia Kühne
Kai Beykirch
Matthias Pfeiffer
Fabian Braunbeck
Basil Vlassaras
Janusch Munkwitz
Matthias Bartsch
Stefan Brenner
Niels Roskamp

The Collective
Oliver Moore
Thorsten Grimm
Thorsten Frank
Patricia Kempf
Christina Fix
Jan Diez
Marc Mettler
Bora Tanay
Christian Kohler
Elmar Mellert
Johannes Östringer
Florian Ehing
DJ Friction
Konstantin Sibold
Leif Müller
Daniel von Bernstorff
Nora Erdle
Leo Papini
Robin Wulff
Erik Sturm
Tanja Maria Thurner
Luzie Marquardt
Steffen Binsch
Lothar Heinrich
Raphael Janzer

The Team
**All of you crazy, helpful, open-minded and busy girls and
boys at the entrance, guarding the door,
behind the bar and running the stage. You are
too many to mention — and too great to be forgotten!**

Thanks. You rock.
Reiner X. Sedelmeier, C.R.

LBBW
ZUBLIN
TEAMS WORK
Wanne
ICON TRASH FOUNDED IN 2005 LIFE SUCCESS PAIN REFLEX LOVE
ROCKER 33

Impressum / Colophon

Diese Publikation erscheint anlässlich der Ausstellung/
This publication was published to accompany the exhibition
Rocker 33 — The Years 2005–2011

Herausgeber / Editors
Christian Schiller, David Spaeth, Matthias Straub

Konzept & Kreativdirektion / Concept & Creative Direction
Christian Schiller (Gold & Wirtschaftswunder, www.gww-design.de)

Fotografie / Photography
David Spaeth (www.davidspaeth.com)
Danke an / thanks to Leo Papini
(S. 36, S. 40, S. 49, S. 67, S. 68, S. 96, S. 136, S. 140, S. 151)

Redaktion & Text / Editorial Stuff & Text
Matthias Straub (Studio Malo)

Gestaltung / Design
Sebastian Zimmerhackl, Steffen Hotel (www.selam-x.com)

Lithografie / Lithography:
Wagnerchic Postproduction & Retouching (www.wagnerchic.com)

Übersetzung & Lektorat / Translation & Copy-Editing:
Neil O'Sullivan

Projektmanagement / Project Management, Kerber Verlag:
Verena Simon

Die Deutsche Nationalbibliothek verzeichnet diese Publikation in der
Deutschen Nationalbibliografie; detaillierte bibliografische Daten sind im Internet über
http://dnb.dnb.de abrufbar.
The Deutsche Nationalbibliothek lists this publication in the Deutsche
Nationalbibliografie; detailed bibliographic data are available on the Internet
at http://dnb.dnb.de.

Gesamtherstellung und Vertrieb /
Printed and published by:

Kerber Verlag, Bielefeld
Windelsbleicher Straße 166–170
33659 Bielefeld
Germany
T: +49 (0) 5 21/9 50 08-10
F: +49 (0) 5 21/9 50 08-88
info@kerberverlag.com

Kerber, US Distribution
ARTBOOK | D.A.P.
75 Broad Street, Suite 630
New York, NY 10004
T: +1 (212) 627-1999
F: +1 (212) 627-9484

KERBER Publikationen sind weltweit in ausgewählten
Buchhandlungen und Museumsshops erhältlich (Vertrieb in Europa,
Asien, Süd- und Nordamerika).
KERBER publications are available in selected bookstores and
museum shops worldwide (distributed in Europe, Asia, South and North America).

ISBN 978-3-7356-0567-2
www.kerberverlag.com

Printed in Germany